# SUNSHINE

*and*

# SHADOWS

*Reflections of a
Macmillan Nurse*

---

*by*

Clare Fitzgibbon

## DEDICATION

*I dedicate this book to my husband and three sons,
whose unconditional love and support I treasure
and to my daughters-in-law and grand-children
who give me enormous pleasure.*

*'I have seen flowers come in stony places,*
*And kind things done by men with ugly faces,*
*And the gold cup won by the worst horse at the races.*
*So I trust too.'*

**John Masefield 1878-1967**

★  ★  ★

Published by Encircling Publications:
86 Station Road, Hatfield, Doncaster DN7 6QL
Tel/Fax: 01302 846532
Email: encircling@btopenworld.com   www.edupub.org

Front cover photograph supplied by kind permission of Jackie Pepper

ISBN: 978-0-9556140-0-2

Designed and Printed by Impact Graphics, 9 Atlas Way, Carlisle Street, Sheffield S4 7QQ
Email: martin1print@yahoo.com   Tel: 0114 249 3000  Fax: 0114 249 3001

# Contents

# Foreword

## by Dr Sheila Cassidy

It's hard for today's young doctors and nurses to imagine caring for people without the help of palliative care teams and Macmillan specialist nurses. I ask you to bear with me therefore, while I sketch out a brief scenario of what it used to be like prior to the caring revolution of the late 1970's and early 80's.

An elderly man: we can call him Jo, is suffering from lung cancer which has spread to his bones and he is in agony every time he moves. The doctor has given him morphine which helps the pain a bit so he increases the dose several times. After a few days Jo is no longer clear minded, 'away with the fairies' as his family puts it. From being a dignified elderly man, he becomes a nightmare to nurse, falling out of bed and incontinent.

The doctor comes again and gives him a tranquilliser and increases the morphine further. At last Jo is quiet though he whimpers in agony each time his wife or the district nurse changes his bed. Eventually he slips into a coma and dies. The family are grateful to the doctors and nurses for they know they did their best for Jo. What they don't realise is that the best is in no way good enough and that Jo's suffering could have been prevented.

This scenario was repeated in private houses, hospitals and nursing homes all over the world until a group of nursing and medical pioneers found a better way to care for the dying.

Enough of my heartbreaking scenario: suffice it to say that mismanaged or unmanaged, death from cancer (and other illnesses) can be a fraught and messy business leaving the family racked with grief, anger and guilt after the person has died.

I was privileged to begin my work with the dying in the 1980's when trail-blazers like Drs Cicely Saunders and Robert Twycross had begun to disseminate the knowledge that they had gained at the bedside.

Cicely Saunders coined the term 'total pain': a mixture of physical, emotional, spiritual and family distress. This sounds so obvious now that it's hard to believe that physical pain was for years the only focus; emotional, spiritual and family distress being deemed beyond the remit of doctors and nurses.

A brief look at the modern management of 'total pain' will illustrate the revolution in care which has come about with the development of palliative care and especially the growth of the Macmillan Nursing Service. The 'right' use of morphine, that is the correct dose for the individual patient, given at regular intervals, has transformed the nightmare of cancer pain and the confusion which follows too much morphine is now seen much less often.

The 'Conspiracy of Silence' in which relatives and health carers thought that it was better to lie than tell a patient that he or she was dying is mostly a thing of the past.

Every man, woman and child has the right to know if they have a mortal illness so that plans may be made and goodbyes said.

Distress in the family is inevitable as members face the loss of their loved one but regular visits from a Macmillan Nurse or other skiled health professional provide an opportunity to express fears and grief. This relationship with the family develops over the weeks and months of a terminal illness, until the nurse is a trusted friend who is involved in, but not overwhelmed by, the family's grief.

Macmillan Nurses have become highly skilled in the management of 'total pain' in the terminally ill and they are a crucial member of the General Practice teams with whom they work.

This book, the rich harvest of many years of caring, provides a heart-warming and inspiring insight into the work of one woman who is clearly proud to have been a Macmillan Nurse. Read on, if you dare: you won't be disappointed!

**Sheila Cassidy**

Plymouth 2007

# Preface

## by Professor Jessica Corner

The first Macmillan nurses were appointed in 1975 at the new Macmillan Unit in Christchurch Hospital. Throughout the 1980's and 1990's, The Macmillan Nurse Appeal provided the means to expand these services rapidly. Now over 30 years later there are more than 3,000 Macmillan nurses and a network of over 4,000 Macmillan professionals in a range of settings and service contexts. This extraordinary development in UK wide healthcare, that has improved the lives of so many people affected by cancer, is founded on the efforts and commitment of people like Clare Fitzgibbon. Clare, and others like her took on, quite literally, the mission to change the way people dying from cancer, were cared for. This was a time when services were underdeveloped, when the network of hospice and palliative care services that exists today had not yet been built. It was also long before cancer networks, our national cancer plans, multi-disciplinary teams, or many of the other developments that are helping to transform cancer services across the UK had been put in place.

My close involvement with Macmillan spans a similar timeframe and I closely identify with the pioneering spirit of individuals like Clare in the work of Macmillan nursing and how we all had to learn the hard way about what is ideal in starting up new services, proving their worth to cost conscious health service managers. I recall how demanding single handed Macmillan nursing services were for these pioneers, how difficult it was to set up and run a service from scratch without any well developed template and how, over time, the necessary support and guidance were put in place. A central task we continue to learn about today.

Clare's account also accords with my own professional journey in that she chooses not to devote much of her memoir to the day to day experience of life as a Macmillan nurse or to the practice of Macmillan nursing. Rather, she reveals her work through the remarkable personal journeys of the individuals she met, facing their own death, and the privilege of working alongside them. She also reveals how the boundaries of personal and professional life are continually challenged by such encounters. Like Clare when I think of the things I have learned about my own practice of caring for people who are dying, it is a march of extraordinary individuals who come to mind. What I learned from their particular situations was how to offer therapeutic intervention. It is not the professional strategies, textbook advice or knowledge, but the people.

This book presents a compelling case for why we need to continue with our plans to develop and extend Macmillan services as the Macmillan 'effect' is not yet available to all. There remains much to be done if we are to improve the lives of everyone living with cancer.

**Jessica Corner**

*Director for Improving Cancer Services,*
*Macmillan Cancer Support*

# Introduction

**Sunshine and Shadows** is for anyone who has been or will ever be close to someone who has cancer, for families and friends, for those who have or have had cancer, for health care workers and all those involved in any way with Macmillan Cancer Support.

The author Clare Fitzgibbon began nursing in 1956 when she was eighteen. She was a Macmillan Nurse between 1987 and 1998, commencing at a time when the service was primarily involved with the care of those with advanced stage disease.

**Since then, with enormous advances in the knowledge and treatment of cancer, Macmillan Nurses commonly see patients from the time of diagnosis and often when cure is a strong possibility.**

Clare tells the stories of men and women of all ages, who through their courage, hope, determination, dignity, humour, love and sometimes sheer feistiness spilled sunshine into the shadows of their illness; men and women who allowed her close to travel their journeys with them as a Macmillan Nurse – a role she describes as 'most privileged'.

From those men and women, or their relatives, permission to share these stories has been gladly given although in some cases there was a request that names be changed.

Readers are given insight into how one Macmillan Nurse struggled for survival not only because of the nature of her work, which she describes as challenging and rewarding, but by the sheer volume of work while employed single-handed because of the financial climate at the time. The book tells of people and events before and beyond her years as a Macmillan Nurse, of family, friends and colleagues, and of her sunshine people of Uganda; all she believes contributing to her drive and passion to improve care of all sick; those with cancer, and above all, the care of the dying.

*'As a Macmillan Nurse, I met many more people with cancer than I could possibly mention in this book. For a good number of those I met, it was around the time of their diagnosis, when special, skilled support was required through treatment time. Their treatment was successful and once completed, they wanted to put their whole experience behind them and put their lives back to normal. They certainly didn't want a Macmillan Nurse on their shoulder, but rather tucked away out of sight in their toolbox. Many, I hope will be out there still, never having needed to open their toolbox.*

*Still others I would meet briefly, for advice on a particular aspect of their care. Such patients and families were already receiving the best care possible from their G.P. and District Nurses or Hospice or*

*Nursing Home staff. There would be nothing that a Macmillan Nurse could offer that wasn't already being done.*

*Thankfully more and more patients each year are cured or treated successfully and disappear into the sunset, never needing a Macmillan Nurse again.*

*However the stories I am sharing are mostly about patients who died, for it was by travelling that journey with them, that I came to know them in a special way that would  otherwise never have been possible.'*

The author believes that it is in being close to the dying that we come to know, from them, how best to live.

'When one is able to face the sun then the shadows will always fall behind'.

# Chapter One

## The Sunshine Ball : 1992

*Tomorrow the sunbeams will dance again.*
Eleanor Booth. 1972-1990

I chose a dress the colour of an African sunset. I felt Ellie would have approved.

When the invitation to the Ball first arrived, I had been taken aback at the courage of her parents in wanting to celebrate her life in this way. And yet how like them to want to raise funds to assist others affected by cancer, and to do it in this way.

Now the evening was upon us and the taxi at our front door. My husband smiled as I joined him downstairs. He put an arm around my shoulders.

"Very smooth," he whispered.

"Thanks. You too."

The hotel was the most prestigious in town. A liveried doorman stood in a pool of light greeting a small group of guests who had arrived just ahead of us.

"Brian!" I squeezed his arm as he made to lead me after them. "A minute."

He understood immediately and paused, then turned his

head upwards in the direction I was looking. "A new moon."

"Beautiful isn't she. Like a smile." I walked away a few paces, towards the gardens.

"Yes," he agreed. "And with luck she'll be there all night." He took my hand. "I think we should go in."

Noisy chatter and laughter resounded above a background of string music. Clusters of formally dressed people stood around under bright lights, while others, mostly men, circled an elegant bar placing orders.

I stood briefly on the threshold, feeling far removed from all the glitter and glamour before me. A part of me would like to have slipped away unseen, yet I knew I couldn't do that, for that would be letting someone down. The feeling wasn't in any way foreign to me. Often, I felt inadequate to face certain situations or occasions, but had somehow learned to put on my best face and get on with it. I well remember feeling this way when I was on my way to meet Ellie for the first time.

I had been a few years into my role as a Macmillan Nurse when I received a 'phone call from a specialist at the Cancer Centre. There was a patient of his, aged 17, who he wanted me to see. She had a rare tumour behind one eye, and the treatment she had been receiving for some time had now outlived its usefulness. The tumour was back and he had nothing more to offer. It was only a matter of time. I sensed the defeat in his voice. Ellie had expressed a wish to be cared for at home, but he doubted if this would be possible because of the difficult nature of the tumour and potential problems in controlling pain and other symptoms.

"That said", he added, "she's a remarkable girl. If there's ever anything you think I could do ….." his voice had tailed off. "But her GP knows all that."

Several 'phone calls and a few days later, I was on my way to Ellie's home. Knowing I was coming, at her request, a family gathering had been set up, with her younger brother and sister called home from their boarding schools.

I think I shall always remember that drive out into the Yorkshire Dales that first time. As each mile passed, I prayed that I might have something to offer a family in distress, that I might at least find the right words.

"Clare!" The familiar voice brought me right back into my surroundings.

"Hi, Maureen! How are you?" We hugged, then held each other at arms length, appraising each others dresses, her eyes never quite meeting mine. I remember thinking she was probably doing us both a favour.

"Just fine." She waved an arm. "Isn't this terrific, all these people. And have you seen the tombola? Everyone's been so generous. Brian!" She had spotted him making his way through the crowd. "Over here. How are you?" she asked with all her usual enthusiasm.

"Oh good thanks. And you? And Clifford?"

"We're fine." She smiled broadly. "Now look you two, enjoy yourselves. Have a great evening." She turned to go.

"Can I not get you a drink?" Brian began.

"No, no," adding almost wantonly "or I'll not be able to stand up." She laughed and left us.

I watched as she moved among the crowd, greeting and smiling with friends and acquaintances. She was an attractive woman, younger looking than her years, always dressed and made up well, even on days at home. I only remember seeing her once without make-up. I pushed the broken image from my mind. Instead, I found myself wondering if Ellie would have been more like her mother had she lived; less serious, more fun-loving, but maybe she *had* been before her cancer, before I'd known her.

That is one thing about being a Macmillan Nurse where I feel at a disadvantage. We know our patients and families only when they are faced with serious adversity. I have learned to be on my guard about ever presuming personality types.

I could cite a number of examples where I have thought I had come to know someone, most often a relative and then years later, when outside Macmillan a friendship has developed, I have discovered quite a different person.

There have been incidents during a person's illness when I thought they were acting out of character, when in fact they were doing what they might have done before their illness. I smiled to myself remembering one such incident with Ellie.

"Remind me to tell you a lovely story about Ellie," I whispered to Brian, as some friends came to join us.

Later, as we took our places for dinner in the grand restaurant festooned with balloons and bunting, to the sound of chattering voices and laughter and the tantalising aroma of food, I began to feel nervous. I took the card from my evening bag and the words on it blurred. I swallowed and lifted my eyes to the high ceiling. I blessed the person who taught me that tactic when threatened by tears.

Soon, I was able to bring my gaze back to the room and those around me. I caught Ellie's father looking at me and his flushed benevolent face beamed, his calmness reaching out to me. Beside me, Brian put one hand reassuringly on my arm. I stood up and slowly, like the sea, a wave of silence rippled around the whole room. I took a deep breath and in a surprisingly steady voice said.

*"We are here because of a young girl who brought sunshine into our lives. She would want us to cherish each moment, for the most important is now. So I ask; that this food be blessed and this evening be fun."*

Much later, after an hour of dancing, we went outside for some fresh air and quiet.

"You were going to tell me a funny story," Brian prompted.

"A lovely story," I corrected, " and a sad one. But I guess it is funny too. How did you know?"

"Oh, I could tell from your expression."

"It was not so long before Ellie died, when she used to have a really good day now and then. On one of these, she had been taken for a ride out to a nearby Mill Shop.

Her father's birthday was coming up, so she had her savings with her intending to buy him one of those lovely Beresford china horses."

"When the woman gave me the price," Ellie told me, "it was much more than I had."

Then she had groaned. "Can you believe what I did? I feel so sorry for her now."

"Go on, tell me," I urged, wondering whatever was coming.

"I told her!"

"You told her, Ellie?" I was becoming perplexed and yet I could sense in her voice a mischief as if, though aghast at her own behaviour, she had actually enjoyed whatever it was she had done or said.

"I think it must have been the steroids," she said then. "You know, making me act differently from normal." Then she laughed. "That poor woman. She went really white. But I got my horse."

All this was on the 'phone for she had rung me on returning home. "Well I'm pleased you got your horse," I told her. "Are you going to tell me now what you said?"

"I told her I was dying." There was a moment's silence. "I told her I hadn't enough time to save any more." There followed another brief silence. "Do you think that was really bad of me?"

"No Ellie. Not bad." I found myself wanting to laugh and cry at the same time, but managed to stop the tears. "Steroids can have strange effects," I told her. I have often wondered since if that was Ellie being her real self.

I suspect Brian was also struggling with tears and laughter over the story, for he just held me, until we made our way back in to the Ball to dance some more.

★ ★ ★

That first meeting with Ellie and her family was probably my greatest test. I think I passed it. Generally, a

Macmillan Nurse will meet one or two members of a family at first contact – not six; or eight if you count the dogs! The thought of it had been far more daunting and anxiety-making than the actual experience.

I had come to realise how helpful it was in my work, to have a goal in mind for each visit. This provided me with a sense of direction. I had decided that my goal for this visit should be nothing more than for me to introduce myself and describe my role, and for Ellie and her family to have a look at me and ask any questions.

It was all of that and much more besides. The brave new world of 'telling patients the truth' was upon us at that time, though only partially in practice. Ellie was the first person I had come across who was able to articulate it to me, in front of her family.

There were no histrionics – she just told it how it was, with expressed concern for her family. Her specialist had been right in describing her as 'remarkable'. What he hadn't told me was how very pretty she was. I had never seen her before she lost her beautiful dark hair which I recognised from photos in their lounge. Even with a turban covering her baldness and a dressing over one eye, before me was the same face with the same lovely bone structure, the same endearing smile. Yet change there surely must be and I felt my heart contract with some of the pain her parents would be feeling, watching the effects of cancer and its treatment on their daughter.

My own sons were aged 20, 21 and 22 at the time. Not long after my first encounter with Ellie, when I found two of them, locked in what seemed to me a deadly combat, I remember shouting at them to stop. "Don't you realise people of your age are dying!" It hadn't been appropriate or very helpful at the time. Later, when one of them asked me why I'd got so upset, I had tried to explain.

It is impossible not to take your work home with you when you are dealing with life and death issues and loss in such human costs.

I returned to see Ellie within a week on a warm sunny day. She was dressed and looking out for me." I'd like a walk with you," she told me on my arrival. "Down the fields to the river."

I barely hesitated. "If you're up to it, I'm game." I looked at her mother who was watching us.

"Will I come with you?" she asked.

"No Mum." Ellie replied, almost too quickly.

"Perhaps you could have a nice cuppa ready for us when we get back," I suggested, concerned not to destabilise their relationship in any way.

The family labrador bounded ahead of us on our walk, which wasn't far. We didn't talk much, just now and then Ellie would pause in the meadow of grass and wild flowers. "Lovely isn't it," she would say wistfully, looking around at the gentle sloping dales. In such moments I knew I had to be extra strong. I told myself again, how much we take for granted.

On our return, yet still a short way from the house, she stopped me. "Can we sit here? I need to talk to you."

Once seated, she began in earnest. "Can you please help Mum and Dad? They don't seem to realise I am not going to get better."

I moved up close to her, sensing her distress. "Tell me what ….."

"Well they are still hopeful, still trying, looking for some miracle drug."

"And you, Ellie?"

"I know if there was anything, my specialist would know. Why can't they just accept that."

"Oh Ellie!" I put an arm around her shoulders. "All of this is so hard isn't it."

"You see I don't want them getting their hopes up again. Spending their money and time." She looked at me then directly. "You see I don't know how much time I have. Do you know?"

I shook my head. Now I was holding both her hands in mine. "No, Ellie, I don't," I answered honestly.

"Will you tell me when you know …. When you know it's near."

"It's not always possible," I began "You see…."

"But of all people, you should know. And I really would want to know."

"Okay," I agreed. "I'll try."

She smiled. "You see I have things to sort out." She was looking pale now and suddenly very tired.

"Let's get back for that cuppa," I suggested, helping her up "And then how would you feel when you've had a rest, about talking with your Mum about those things you have to sort out, maybe even making a list. What do you think?"

"I think that is what I shall do."

"And Ellie," I said, ever so gently, "about your Mum and Dad. It seems to me that you are at a different place to them on this journey of your illness." I remember uttering the words so carefully. At times like that, when it turned out right, I felt that the words were somehow being given to me. "They will catch you up, but right now they will do anything, simply because they love you and can't bear the thought of losing you."

★ ★ ★

"It's the last dance," my husband whispered, as the group struck up a dreamy number, the lights dimmed, voices fell and people took to the floor. I shut my eyes, and let Brian lead me, feeling loved and safe in his arms. I found myself thanking God for all that we had in our lives.

Ellie began her list of things she must do and true to her generous nature, it was mostly about giving away her treasured collection of flower fairies, of miniature china cottages, of earrings and other special belongings. While this was painful to watch, it seemed to give her happiness and great peace of mind.

She asked to see the minister of the church where she was to be buried and then planned her own funeral service, more or less, which she wanted to be joyous. For some of us, this was almost too much. For Ellie, it gave her a great sense of pride and achievement.

There were fun things that she wanted to do too. One was to go up in a hot air balloon and she achieved it but not before we gained assurance for her from a physicist that her wig would not be dissolved by the hot air!

Another thing that gave her great joy, was the way in which each member of her family coped, from her young brother who was often close at her side, to her elderly grand-mother whose sorrow was written on her face.

Ellie was, of course only human and because she expected much of herself, so she did of others. Her head-mistress for one came under attack. She visited, yet Ellie always found her visits irksome. "She never refers to my illness," Ellie would complain, "or even asks how I am feeling. She comes into my bedroom and talks of every day goings on, like I wasn't even sick!"

However much I tried to defuse Ellie's anger, that remained one area where I couldn't even budge her. I concluded that it was quite healthy for her to experience anger and to have an outlet for it. Poor woman was probably lost for words in the face of one of her brightest students facing death. At least she didn't stay away altogether.

Through most of her illness Ellie had kept a diary, using it as a sort of sounding board. I believe in some way I became a replacement for that, particularly to do with feelings that she felt were just too painful to talk about with her family.

She certainly had a way with words and I believe would one day have become a writer of some note, had she survived her cancer. She wrote very coherently on the meaning of suffering, and of not being listened to, which she shared with me. Then there was her poem, which she wrote as she faced her own death. I believe it to be one of Ellie's greatest legacies.

## YESTERDAY, TODAY AND TOMORROW

### YESTERDAY

*I watched with wonder*
*As the rosebud burst forth into*
*A vermillion bloom of velveteen petals*

### TODAY

*the thorns prick at my fingertips*
*And the only light is the sullen gleam of my tears*
*The only sound the hollow echoes of my empty world*

### TOMORROW

*the sunbeams will dance again*
*And in the rich soil, the saplings will flourish*
*Beneath the warm golden hue of the new dawn.*

Ellie, I salute you, for allowing me into your short and precious life, for the lessons I learned from knowing you, for being patient with me and my colleagues when we got it wrong, for the laughter we shared, and the tears, and perhaps above all, for this poem and the message of hope it has for each one of us.

# Chapter Two

## Years in the Foothills : from 1956

*There is nothing like returning to a place that remains unchanged to find the ways that you yourself have altered.*

*Nelson Mandela.*

I began my nurse training in 1956, half a century ago. In those days it included all sorts of domestic duties even before, as in my case, one reached the dizzy status of a black-belted, registered nurse. The disposable world was some way off so bedpans, bottles and sputum mugs were of aluminium or stainless steel and were manually cleaned by student nurses. This responsibility was known in my hospital as 'sluice duties'!

Such an assignment did have some advantages in that it provided a temporary safe haven from Sister's scrutiny and an opportunity, when there were two of you, for a gossip and a giggle. I also found it an escape for release of emotions we were not supposed to have. Many a newly polished bedpan has been streaked with my tears. Nurses like men, were not expected to cry. I did then, I have since and I still do and I don't believe my tears have ever done anyone any harm, except temporarily to my face!

I went into nursing because I wanted to help people who were sick to get better. I don't believe at that time I had faced the fact that many don't recover and it was in my second year when a colleague and friend became very sick. She had recurrent sore throats making her very pale and tired-looking, though our Nurses' Doctor and Home Sister remained seemingly unconcerned and certainly unsympathetic. Eventually she collapsed on duty and, after a series of tests, was admitted to the infectious diseases unit out on the edge of town. We, her friends, speculated over her diagnosis, but were told that in an effort to protect her from infection, we must not visit.

I was working on a Medical Ward at the time and one afternoon, was told by Sister to prepare a side-room for a new patient with leukaemia. While one couldn't afford time to stand around awaiting the arrival of a new patient, one always kept an eye and an ear on the alert. Just as soon as I heard a trolley at the swing doors of the ward, I hurried the length of the Florence Nightingale unit.

"Here, Mac," urged Archie the porter as I got near "give us a hand." He was struggling to hold the doors open and manoeuvre the trolley through, while trying to shield the bottle of blood transfusion, swinging precariously from a short pole fixed to one side.

"You all right, pet?," I heard him say to the patient as I reached the doors, just in time to prevent them swinging shut and banging against the trolley. Archie was quite the kindest person I knew but how I wished that just now and again, he would stop to think and ask for help before a calamity occurred.

Then I turned to greet our new patient and stopped, frozen in my every movement. "I'm sorry," a soft voice whispered. "I didn't mean to shock you."

"Oh no, no, Roma," I stuttered. "You, you didn't. It's just nobody told me." I moved to her side and smiled down at her. She brought her free arm from under the covers and I took her cold hand and held it between mine. Her dark, Italian eyes seemed to have taken over her face, her clear, pale skin was now ashen, framed by her dark, beautiful hair. I wanted to say something, but my mouth felt strange, as if it didn't belong to me.

"I'm so glad you're here," she whispered.

"Me too," I managed, believing it, but at the same time terrified.

Back then, in the 1950s, we didn't have the experience, knowledge or understanding of diseases that we have today, nor the treatments but I believe our care for Roma was the best at that time. For me it was an immediate thing, in the here and now, bathing, changing, manicuring, anything to make her comfortable, with her mother assisting whenever she was there. We never discussed her condition or the future. Naïve as it must sound, I don't believe we even thought about it; until the day everything began to go horribly wrong.

I was in the side-room with Roma when her condition changed dramatically before my eyes. She became shocked, cold, clammy and gasping for breath. I rang the bell.

Sister came and within an hour, two of our doctors had another blood transfusion going and she was definitely picking up. Her mother had arrived to sit with her, freeing me to get on with other pressing, ward duties.

Sometime later, she wanted a bedpan and I knew her condition had worsened again. Sister told me to phone for the doctor.

"It's time you called the priest," he said coldly. "We've done all we can."

I was outraged! How could he? How dare he? For a long time, I felt only hate in my heart for that man. Over the years, I came to realise that he knew no other way of breaking bad news, that he too must have been feeling defeated. Nevertheless, it took me a long, long time to forgive him. I believe I grew up overnight, but not in the way I would choose for anyone else.

I remember telling Sister what the doctor had said. She went with me to Roma's room, suggested her mother wait outside and instructed me to 'sit tight'. I moved close to my friend and sat on the edge of her bed.

Roma looked straight at me. "I'm dying," she said simply, clutching my hand. Blood was trickling down both her nostrils. "Please tell them I love them," she gasped, "my mother, my father," again she gasped for air "all my family," she managed a half smile, her face now colourless "and you."

She moved to sit forward as if to be able to find breath. I tried to help by supporting her, one arm around her shoulders, the other holding her head against mine. Tears were streaming down my face. "And we all love you too," I got out, as she died in my arms.

I brought her mother in and she kissed her daughter and held her and asked me to stay awhile with her before calling Sister.

The loss of my friend and the way she died had a profound effect upon me. I knew it didn't have to be that way, with no communication between professionals on the team, or with Roma and her family, with no opportunity to say things she may have wanted to say, and with her mother outside the door. There had to be better ways than that!

In those days there had been little exploration, let alone research, into feelings or even psycho-social effects of illness or loss, on individuals or families. There are still those today who consider such aspects 'soft' or unnecessary; thankfully they are in the minority.

Through the specialty of Palliative Care, patient 'care' has become as important as 'cure'. Books are available on 'Breaking Bad News', communication skills are included in the training of health care workers, and the word 'holistic'- attending to the psychological, social, spiritual, cultural and physical needs of the individual – appears across every spectrum.

I believe, like some others of that era, I was born with an awareness of the need to consider the whole person, physically and psychologically, and so it was natural for me to use that approach.

I found myself drawn to patients who were close to death. I came to know who they were because they would be moved, either into a side-room or to the top of the ward, nearest Sister's office, often with their screen curtain half drawn. At doctors' rounds, they were most often passed by or spoken of in whispers at the foot of their bed.

I ached for them. If I were dying I would not want to feel abandoned, or written off, discarded. I was convinced patients in our care must be feeling this in the way we behaved towards them.

"How do you feel," I would ask gently, risking Sister's wrath "about being moved here?" At times, such a question would open up communication, enabling patients to explore areas so far closed to them and sometimes, this would lead to patient choice in matters of their future care and treatment.

Nurses then were not supposed to 'waste time' sitting with patients. On reflection now, I know I did not do enough during those years to bring about the change that was needed in care of the dying in our hospitals. I do know that I never felt uncomfortable in getting alongside them. Rather, I felt privileged that they would welcome my approach and the opportunity to talk, which I would encourage while often just listening, which alone seemed to bring them great comfort.

After qualifying as a registered nurse, I had a wide and varied experience, during which I am happy to say, most patients recovered and got well. I then went on to do my midwifery training which I loved. I still feel every birth to be a miraculous event, even while knowing it to be a perfectly natural phenomenon.

When I was 26, I experienced a strong call of altruism. This followed a TV documentary on health conditions for people living in sub-Saharan Africa. For the first time I was struck by how much we had in our world compared with others. I was working then as a Sister in the operating theatre of a very well resourced hospital, where of late, a petty rancour had developed within the team with which I wanted no part. I saw this as an indication that it was time to move on.

★ ★ ★

## A Call to Foreign Lands: April 1964

Uganda in the sixties, after independence, was considered a stable and safe place for a single white woman to be. This fact did little to allay fears that my parents had about  their daughter ending up in a cauldron for someone's next meal! Nevertheless, I was quietly proud of their gesture in accompanying me to the dockside to see me set sail for the African continent.

Thanks to Crown Agents, for responding to my request to travel by sea rather than by air, I then had a most memorable three weeks holiday. With my past behind me and my future someway off, I had only the now to enjoy, and I did, free from all responsibility. We docked at Mombasa, Kenya and there followed a two day journey by train to Kampala, the capital of Uganda. After an overnight stay there, I was collected and taken by Ministry car on a three and a half hour journey up country to my destination, Mbarara. Winston Churchill had called Uganda the 'Pearl of Africa' and I began to see why, as I was driven, surprisingly, on a tarmac road, through swamps, forests, rolling hills and rich, fertile valleys. The people we saw along the roadside and in the fields wore bright, colourful clothes and as they waved to us, I began to feel this was going to be one amazing adventure. The reality of my work place was something else!

First sight of the hospital was good. Single-storey, cream painted buildings with corrugated-iron roofs stood in grounds graced by tall trees and flowering shrubs. Blue skies and sunshine enhanced the scene, as did the uniformed workers and visitors outside the wards, who called friendly greetings to each other.

Once inside, I was shocked to see that the Outpatient area was full to overflowing with a mass of sick-looking people waiting to be seen; some lying on the stone floor, others sitting sideways on wooden benches, squashed up against each other like a disorderly row of sardines. Children whimpered, adults moaned and an over-whelming stench of sickness mingled with the strong distinctive scent of disinfectant.

The ward areas had an air of order and cleanliness about them, but with the exception of the Maternity Ward, all were seriously overcrowded with floor patients between each bed. There was an absence of bed linen. Most patients lay between dark blankets and where there were pillows, they were uncovered, their striped calico the only contrast against the dark blankets. One or two patients on every ward had their own sheets, and embroidered covers for their bedside cupboards, clear indicators of their social status.

I was shown the children last – for in reality there was no Children's Ward. One of the two Medical Wards served as a makeshift, but with no cots and very little bed linen. Only the biggest children or those with severe burns had a bed to themselves. Mostly it was three to a bed, lying horizontally, their mothers sleeping on the floor under or between the beds.

I slept badly that night, wondering what I was doing here and whether I should try now for the next 'plane home. Those thoughts were fleeting for I stayed and like to think I made a difference. My time in Uganda certainly made a difference to me, for when I did leave some eight and a half years later, my single status had changed to one of wife and mother!

I have enough stories in my memories from that time to fill another book; it is only possible here to give you a flavour. My working life as one of three Nursing Sisters at the two hundred and fifty-bedded hospital was such a contrast to everything I had known before that it was almost beyond imaginings. Yet the common threads were there, people who were sick need caring for and generally speaking, those who choose that caring career are compassionate in nature and given the right training, acquire the necessary skills. The huge gap which I discovered there lay in the often total absence of the necessary resources.

In my first week in Mbarara there was a call for blood transfusions which just could not be met. The blood bank was completely empty following a bad, road traffic accident where several victims had required blood and the Medical Assistant, who looked over this service, was away sick. Could I accompany someone to the Prison to collect some? A few hours later, we returned with around twelve units of blood in exchange for a crate of Pepsi and some cigarettes! The result – a few more lives saved. When the situation repeated itself at Christmas, before we had a full functioning service established, I got quite a reputation when I went into the Sports Club and persuaded a couple of golfers to donate their probably over-the-limit blood.

Of prime concern to me, was the absence of cots where very sick children could be nursed. We may take it as a matter of course that a child needs a cot and generally some form of push chair; not so in Uganda and most African countries where children sleep on a mat and get transported around on a back or a hip. On asking around, I was told that there was a white man running a rural trade school just out of town who might make me some cots. He did and a couple of years later became my husband!

In 1964 there was still a level of severe malnutrition in Uganda which presented in the form of merasmus and/or kwashiorkor, both images I had only seen on television, in the skinny limbed and swollen bellied or pale skinned and light haired of refugee camps; yet here they were, patients in our hospital, eyes dull in their miserable little faces staring up at me from the floor or their mothers' laps. In time, working with others, we developed a successful recovery programme for these children which included nutrition training for their families, some of whom had somehow missed out on the importance of protein for weaned children, even though they often grew it and fed it to the rest of the family. Towards the end of my second year, the hospital got its very own Children's Ward, which was a great day for Mbarara.

During that period of time Tuberculosis was highly prevalent, due partly to the high consumption of milk from untreated cattle and environmental characteristics such as overcrowded living conditions, poverty, malnu-trition and the inevitable lack of compliance with regular drug taking as individuals began to feel better. This resulted in TB wards being constantly full beyond capacity, spilling out on to open verandas exposed to tropical downpours during the rainy season. To alleviate this situation we worked together to push the programme for community care which did become and remains, a model to this day.

Around that time there was a rabies outbreak which demanded the very best from everyone, yet presented great challenges when staff fearful of being infected from a victim's saliva sought to desert their posts; mostly compassion and goodwill won through.

In contrast to my working life, after marriage and arrival of our family, life was fun and with the kind climate, we did things we could never have done in England. Playing in the garden all year round and more adventurously, camping with our boys under canvas in the game reserve or by the side of the Indian Ocean, albeit after a drive of nearly nine hundred miles, were truly wonderful experiences. Yes, life was good for us and we believed, getting steadily better for Ugandans – until, that is, the tables turned.

As our 'plane sat on the runway at Entebbe Airport, I wept silently for the people of Uganda who had become our friends, work colleagues and companions in life, and who we were now leaving behind to face their fate under the reign of General Idi Amin.

★ ★ ★

*Back Home: November 1972*

Had I still been single, or childless, I might have stayed on in Uganda, but with three small boys under the age of five my husband and I knew that, for their safety at that time, we had no choice but to leave Uganda.

Within three months, we had a roof of our own over our heads, my husband a full-time teaching post and I was back to nursing in England, for two nights a week in the local hospital.

On my second night, I was assigned to a busy, male surgical ward, specifically to admit two new patients, while a recently qualified Staff Nurse and a student tended to ward duties and settled patients for the night. When all was calm sometime after midnight, I volunteered to cover for the Staff-Nurse while she went for a short break.

"Just give me a run down of the patients before you go." I requested.

"No problem," she replied. "This is my fifth consecutive night, so I know them all well now." With impressive competence, she gave me a thumbnail sketch of each one of the twenty patients in the main ward, indicating those I should keep under special observation.

"And what about the end side-room?" I asked, where I had noticed a curtain across the porthole window.

"Oh, Mr Smith's in there. But he's dying, so there's nothing to be done there." My heart sank to my flat-soled shoes. I felt somewhere between screaming and weeping. This was 1973! Had nothing changed in the nine years I had been away?

Before dawn broke Mr Smith died, not alone but with his son and daughter-in-law sitting with him.

As my anger and anguish subsided, I talked with the young staff nurse and student about our care of the dying and their increased need for human contact. Not long after this, that same Staff Nurse came to ask me if I would lead a discussion among her peers, which she had arranged, to form a 'Care of The Dying' group within the hospital. Such a suggestion was music to my ears!

As our family adjusted to life back in Britain and became involved in the community, I was drawn into membership of an organisation 'for lively – minded women who wanted to explore issues other than babies and the price of fish'. How horribly snobbish that sounds to me today! Healthcare was high on the agenda and in particular, cervical and breast cancer. It was in the very early days of pap smears and long before there was a National Breast Screening programme.

Following the death of one of its members, the group had a visiting speaker, one Betty Westgate, founder of Breast Cancer Care then known as The Mastectomy Association. She greatly inspired us with her own story of breast cancer and how through it, a helpline had been set up offering callers support and encouragement. As a result, with others who had been motivated to do something, I became a founder member of the first northern branch of the Women's National Cancer Control Campaign. (WNCCC) This was an educational charity to encourage women to have regular cervical smear tests and to become breast aware through Breast Self Examination.

I went to the Christie Hospital in Manchester for training in preparation for giving talks about cancer and the importance of early detection. With a working committee formed by now, some local publicity and an eagerness to spread the word, a busy programme of talks was soon underway, shared between three nurse members.

I have wondered since how different life might have been if I had been a more traditional housewife and mother, without this drive to campaign for change where I felt there was need or injustice. I do hope our children were never neglected because of it, though I suspect they inherited some of my genes which may account for the drive they each have in their working lives. Thankfully, they each have compassion and concern for others, and as importantly, have some of their father's genes too in their good natured and fun-loving personalities, their keen sporting interests and their faithfulness.

I would not want any readers to think that my life was one of sacrifice in this voluntary work, for on the contrary, I got an enormous buzz from talking to groups about cancer; imparting knowledge, reducing fears, providing opportunities for questions and encouraging early visits to GPs for those with worrying symptoms. In essence, giving people control over their lives.

What struck me above all else at that time, was that after every talk, there was always one, and often two or more, who came to tell me about someone close to them, who had died from cancer. Invariably, though they often spoke of the distress from delayed diagnosis, their residual grief was about the unresolved pain of the deceased. It seemed to me it was not only the loss causing distress in these bereaved, but rather the way their loved one had died, in pain both physical and psychosocial.

I became troubled by this and spoke of it to the two doctors who had become associated with WNCCC, a local General Practitioner and a Professor of Radiotherapy. Here I was, speaking publicly about cancer and the importance of early detection, while those with first-hand experience were burdened with memories of uncontrolled pain and poor, or no, meaningful communication. I believe I was hearing stirrings of what was abroad at that time, an increased awareness by others for others, particularly in relation to life-threatening illness.

During the seventies, the modern hospice movement was growing, inspired by its founder, the late Cicely Saunders, who died in 2005. Dame Cicely, as she became, was twenty- nine and a hospital almoner when she fell in love with David, a patient dying from an incurable form of cancer. It was 1947 at that time and incurable patients received very little special care in hospitals. Doctors were trained to cure and anyone who could not be cured, represented a failure. Such patients were often left alone in constant pain; others heavily drugged to deaden the pain, so half asleep until they died.

Before David died, he and Cicely talked about the need for more loving care and for research into pain control. And so the idea was born for a special hospital for the terminally ill. This young man made his will and left her £500. "I'll be a window in your home," he told her.

Cicely was already a trained nurse, but a doctor friend told her, "If you really want to change things, go ahead and read medicine. It's the doctors who desert the dying."

She qualified in 1958 and following years of very hard work, research, writing and lecturing about care of the dying and massive fundraising, St Christopher's Hospice in Sydenham, London was opened in 1967, with a window in the entrance dedicated to David.

Others slowly followed wherever monies could be raised around Britain. The Hospice movement stirred into life; developments in nursing became visible, a deepening awareness of human wholeness was awakening as new seedlings in the first rains after a drought. The NHS was taking note and in my own area a Working Group was set up to consider care of the dying. I was invited to join and this provided a very valuable forum where care came under scrutiny and where voices of the bereaved could be heard. This was one of several events occurring around that time, which unwittingly, were leading me through the foothills, to a base camp from where I would set off for the summit of my career as a Macmillan Nurse.

## A Break from Nursing: 1978-81

Five years' night duty had taken its toll and I wanted more time with our young family; also to co-found a local Cruse Bereavement Service, to further my cancer education activities, which by now had extended to a support role for women newly diagnosed with breast cancer, and to pursue my creative writing. During this time, an uncle of mine was dying from cancer at his home in the south of England. During 'phone-calls, my aunt told me a Macmillan Nurse was visiting.

"Without her, he'd have had to go into hospital or a hospice," she explained, "and none of us wanted that."

"What exactly does she do?" I remember asking.

"She listens," she told me, "to both of us, and to the children. She explains things. And she advises on his pain and other problems. I can't tell you the difference she is making."

I remember writing to Macmillan Cancer Support then known as The National Society for Cancer Relief, wanting to know how we could have Macmillan Nurses in our area. My letter was passed to Anne, one of their earliest nurses, who became my role model and very good friend.

*Back to Nursing. 1981*

The early eighties saw me back to part-time nursing on days, in Out-Patient Clinics, most importantly in Oncology (cancer). I thought I would miss the bedside nursing, instead I became acutely aware of the needs of patients attending oncology clinics.

My training had been ongoing throughout my career and cancer counselling and bereavement were carefully chosen priorities.

I became hugely excited on learning there was a recommendation for a Macmillan Service in our District. Unfortunately, however, at that time there was an attitude afoot among some professionals in key positions in the District to oppose this. They were open in their opposition, going as far as being quoted in the local press. I was inwardly outraged but old enough to see this for what it was. Some doctors and nurses saw the recommendation as a direct criticism of their care, others welcomed it as a way forward for better patient care. I knew I must play my part in finding another route to achieve what I knew to be needed.

My fervour may have waned, had I not had a close and personal experience which only served to empower me further, and to influence others. A dear friend, mother of four children, who had been battling with cancer, was becoming extremely ill. Despite her family and friends' best efforts and those of her doctor, district nurse and priest, her pain and distress were overwhelming us. We all knew we needed specialist help.

A Macmillan Nurse from the neighbouring district was contacted and given permission to visit. She made the difference we had all been hoping for and also left her contact details so we could speak with her when difficulties arose again.

It still took four long years, after my friend's death in 1982, to persuade the Health Authority that the care of patients with cancer could be improved with the introduction of a Macmillan Service.

The frontiers in the treatments of cancers were by now far advanced from the late fifties when my friend Roma had died, and continued to be pushed steadily forward. Macmillan Nurses, who had been introduced for 'the care of the dying cancer patient', were changing their role to one of 'cancer nurse specialist'.

A local Consultant in Haematology carried out a study among hospital nursing staff, which indicated clearly, that the majority felt a Macmillan Nurse would benefit patient care. Local fund-raising began in earnest among Macmillan supporters. Few realise that though Macmillan seed fund for the first three years of a new post, the nurse is employed by the NHS Trust.

Interviews took place late in the year of 1986. I was not the candidate selected and after picking up my bruised pride and disappointment, I rejoiced that while we could hardly claim to have a service with only one nurse, at long last we had our very own Macmillan Nurse. Some months into the new and difficult post, the appointee decided on a move somewhere closer to her home. Second time around, in July 1987 I was appointed.

I had finally reached base camp and my task now lay ahead, knowing that I could climb the mountain, but only if others came along with me.

I had always known that the first year as a Macmillan Nurse would be tough and it was – very tough.

Before going on to tell you something of that, I want to share the stories of two families in our community affected by cancer before I became a Macmillan Nurse, and how those experiences impacted on me and on our family.

# *Chapter Three*

## Families in Loss : 1980s

> *In the bearing of another's burdens, in the sharing of another's pain, we begin to dance.*
>
> *Jim Cotter*

When you are in the midst of something personal and traumatic, at the time it is happening, you do what you can, rarely pausing to look above the parapet and consider the consequences. Even if I had it wouldn't have changed anything.

It had not occurred to me that the painful exposure of our whole family to the loss within another family, could be preparing each one of us for the work I was to become involved with as a Macmillan Nurse. In much broader terms, for our young sons I believe the experience helped shape them into the caring, compassionate individuals they are today.

It is more than twenty years now since our friend Pauline died, leaving behind boy and girl twins of ten years, daughters of fourteen and sixteen and a husband.

Not long since, in an email from one of her girls, I received what I consider to be one of the greatest compliments ever. *'I know that God sent you as a replacement of Mum in my life, please always know that I hold*

*you in as high regard as I would have her, and you will always
hold a very special place in my heart.'*

There have been times in my life when I have thought
seriously about the great master plan. If a God does exist
as a great force of good and love in the world, maybe he
did have a hand in me and my family coming to know
Pauline and her family.

So many times I have openly questioned how a loving
God could allow this or that to happen. Far less often
have I openly acknowledged the belief I have that such
a God does exist and does work in mysterious ways for
good in the world. My own journey in spirituality
continues. In my efforts to be non-judgemental and to
embrace believers and non-believers alike, especially in
my work as a Macmillan Nurse, I could be accused by
some, of failing in my silent witness. I have a fear of
offending others, of appearing arrogant, or dare I say it,
of appearing naïve in our present secular society.

What is true is that Pauline was in my life all too briefly.
We first met when she and her family came to live in our
area, from East Africa. They chose our town in order to
be close to her sister and family, and her parents. We
struck up an immediate attachment. We discovered we
had things in common in that we had both met our
husbands overseas, married and had our children there;
but it went much deeper than that. We found we shared
the same values, laughed at the same things and soon
became each other's confidantes.

They bought a house only five minutes' walk away from
ours. We became close as families. They were adjusting to
life in the UK and facing many of the difficulties we had
faced less than ten years previously. There were new

discoveries too. I well remember being in their home one evening when Pauline was putting away the supermarket shopping. "Look what I've discovered," she'd said with glee. "Pot noodles! You just add boiling water and hey presto, a snack for hungry children." We had laughed together and I'd teased her about making money in television advertising.

When her father became ill with cancer, a great sadness came upon her and all the family. Then came Pauline's own diagnosis of cancer, which was devastating. It felt so unfair, made all the worse when her father died. Despite her very positive attitude, not for her the disease-free period after treatment that thankfully so many experience today, but an unrelenting advance. Her symptoms at times were nothing short of cruel, necessitating admissions to hospitals and separation from her family. Her sister and mother were stoic in their support, her husband too; her children baffled and bewildered at what was happening to their mother. As a friend and nurse, I felt fear; as a family we tried to help in whatever ways we could. Pauline herself remained optimistic, determined to conquer her disease.

I have in my mind an incident that is as fresh as if it happened yesterday. Our two families attended the same church at the time, and one Sunday morning as we met outside, Pauline turned to us. "We're always asking things of God," she said with exasperation. "Look at the Lord's Prayer. Give us this …. Forgive us that …." She opened her arms expressively. "How often do we thank him? Praise him?"

"Sure." I nodded, wondering what had made her so agitated.

"So today, I have asked for nothing," she told us. "I've just thanked him."

There was a poignancy about her mood that day that I can still recall, as if she was telling me something deeply meaningful. It felt a bit like the time she asked to begin writing her Christmas cards, even though it was only October as if she knew something we didn't. With hindsight and experience of Macmillan nursing, perhaps I should have explored her remarks further that day.

I do believe, among those of us who were looking after her when she became bedridden, that we did allow for openness while still living in hope that her illness would take a U turn back towards recovery. I remember one of the saddest tasks I was called upon to do, standing with her mother behind the closed cellar door, trying to help her accept that time was fast running out.

I never again want to feel the overwhelming sadness for Pauline's whole family that I experienced the night she died. I was in the bathroom, my head bowed over the sink, when my nurse friend came to me and touched me deeply by acknowledging my loss too, as Pauline's friend. I remember much later that night, tucking each of the children into their beds except for Suzie who didn't want to be upstairs, so we lay together on the floor of the lounge under a blanket until first light. I still recall the scrambled eggs that her twin brother made for our breakfast and the walk to town with them both the following day, and one of them saying, "Don't they know my mum has died?" at sight of people going about their ordinary business.

I remember how brave my own sons were when they said they would like to go with Brian and me, to see

Pauline's body in the Chapel of Rest, and how lovely her face was again, free from the pain that had ravaged it. Forever imprinted on my memory are the faces of her children as they stood around her grave and courageously, one by one, stepped forward to make their final farewells each with a single rose. I remember the face of her husband and of my own husband and those of our sons and the palpable sadness that dwelt within our family at that time. There are other memories, some too painful to disturb from their place under the tears and leaves that fell that autumn.

In the years between, though I have had no Pauline as a friend, I have known so much joy from her children, especially her girls who have been to us like the daughters we never had, and to our sons, the sisters they may have liked. We have shared so much fun and laughter during their growing up. We have also shared worries and heartache when things have gone wrong. If in some small way I have been there for them as their mother may have hoped, I am deeply grateful for the love they have returned a thousand fold. I ask nothing from them or for them, save their health and their happiness. Each one of them has overcome so much. I know their mother would be as proud of them as I am, and as I know their father to be, and believe the same to be true of their step-mother.

It would be remiss of me not to mention here the very difficult role that step parents take on in such circumstances. It is seldom if ever easy, as they strive to walk that sensitive and difficult of paths. So much understanding from all parties is required and this is so often a scarce commodity, particularly in children and young adults who have lost a parent. Mercifully, this usually develops with maturity as all family members come to accept their loss and, eventually, this new person in their lives.

★  ★  ★

Because it was through Pauline that I had my first 'in-the-flesh' experience of a Macmillan Nurse, I want to share the following descriptive verse – author anon – that was around at that time and much of which I would suggest, still stands today.

*Being a Macmillan Nurse is:*

> *To be without uniform…or a surname…..to be different!*
>
> *To be a colleague – a fellow professional with the district sister, the general practitioner, priest or minister.*
>
> *To share in care!*
>
> *To' let go' the feeling of power, of status … in order to be there for the patient and family.*
>
> *To be obsessed by constipation!*
>
> *To know emotional and professional pain*
>
> *To be vulnerable*
>
> *To recognise grief in all its many forms*
>
> *To know the healing of laughter in unlikely situations*
>
> *To touch…when words are useless*
>
> *To be the advocate for the patient and the carers*
>
> *To know the 'glow' of knowing pain is controlled and a family is at peace*
>
> *To ask for …… NOW!*
>
> *To struggle to read the non-verbal clues in an encounter – with a patient, a carer or a colleague*
>
> *To grieve for the friends we have made through our work*
>
> *To be grateful for what we learn of courage and love.*

My first sharp memory of Peter is as he stood beside his mother at the church door, while we mourners filed past, offering condolences on the untimely death of George, late husband of Dorothy, father of Peter. I remember being struck by how tall he was for a boy of only ten and how brave, while feeling a sharp sense of anguish for him and for his mother.

I had met George a couple of years previously when looking for a suitable venue for a talk on women's cancers. He was churchwarden of a beautiful old, centrally sited building in our town and readily agreed to their hall being used, waiving any fee, telling me his wife had had cancer some years back and wished us well in our work.

Discovering they lived very close to us, I had then met with his wife on a few occasions and we had compared notes on our three sons, and their single adopted son, Peter, who was four years older than our eldest.

George's illness had been vicious and brief, an aggressive form of acute leukaemia which never responded to treatment and cost him his life within a span of only six months.

Along with Dorothy's family and friends, I tried to support her after George's death and we became quite close, though I saw little of Peter except when our two families went out together for Sunday lunch. On the surface he appeared a very polite, cheerful teenager who our sons looked up to, which did cause me minor concern for I saw him as a somewhat indulged boy; but little wonder under the circumstances. This was back in the 1970s when my understanding of the needs of bereaved children was very sketchy, though I do remember alarm bells ringing when I asked Dorothy if he spoke much about his father.

"He doesn't" she'd replied, "and he tells his friends he's away on business." She sighed, before adding hastily as if in defence, "I think he wants to appear normal, doesn't want anyone to feel sorry for him."

When I tentatively suggested that he might benefit from talking with someone about this, she didn't think that was a good idea at all. In matters concerning Peter, I had come to know that I must step very carefully with Dorothy, to avoid offending or upsetting her.

Now past forty, Peter does not recall ever really understanding what was going on at the time, except that he noticed excessive bruising on his father's arms and then suddenly he was in hospital. He remembers being told he was going to get better and believing that, while suspecting from the horrible deterioration in his appearance, that this could not be.

He says running away from what was happening helped, and remembers endless sporting activities, soccer, rugby, basketball or cricket, which he played incessantly during the final stages and after his father's death.

When Dorothy's cancer returned a few years later, she was adamant that she didn't want Peter to know. She loved him, wished to protect him and any suggestions to the contrary were instantly crushed. "Don't you think he has had enough already," she would challenge me, "without burdening him unnecessarily with this." He must have been around fifteen by then and she was able to conceal her regular visits to the hospital and her own doctor by always arranging them during school times, or by cursory reference to routine check-ups.

Within a further two years, Dorothy had deteriorated markedly. No longer was her disease being controlled by the hormone therapy and her mobility was now seriously affected. Her specialist painted a grim picture to her GP who discussed the situation with Dorothy. They wanted to admit her while she received a trial on a new treatment. Peter was seventeen by now, in sixth form and she shared her dilemma with me. After empathising with her situation, I risked her wrath and told her that she must talk with Peter, before any decisions could be arrived at.

"He knows," she whispered dejectedly.

I was not nursing just then, having taken time out to pursue my writing and we lived in a spacious old town house with room to spare. Our sons were excited at the idea of Peter moving in, for eleven, twelve, and thirteen year olds are not averse to a little hero-worship! Dorothy, ever considerate, initially resisted, worried that the extra work entailed in nursing her and having a fourth teenager in our home, would be all too much. Brian and I assured her that between us we would manage, so we should at least give it a try.

On reflection, having responded compassionately to Dorothy's situation, I then went into practical, organiser mode with Peter, unconsciously pulling a blind down on the psychological effects of this trauma and upheaval in his life. I have reproached myself many times for this and once with Peter, seeking his forgiveness, though I don't believe he felt it necessary.

When I railed at the disorderly way Peter left the bathroom or didn't appear for Sunday lunch until hours after the agreed time, our sons understandably rallied to his defence. I made no allowance for the fact that, as an only child, he had never been encouraged to clean up after himself or grasp the importance of coming together at meal times. I think the final straw came when a quite freakish coincidence occurred and he and my husband had sports injuries to their ankles, making both temporarily non-weight bearing and on crutches. Brian made arrangements to be picked up daily so that he could carry on his teaching commitment; not so Peter who considered it a great opportunity to skip school and laze around at home!

I consoled myself that the soundproofing in our home protected Dorothy, who was bed-ridden at the time, from hearing any of my upbraiding of her son. She was the perfect English patient, gracious, considerate, never demanding and mostly comfortable, despite her daily round trips to the cancer centre some seventeen miles away, to which I or one of her friends drove her.

By the end of six weeks, Dorothy was showing a remarkable response to her treatment and was looking to returning home. This became possible when her cousin and husband from Australia stopped off from their 'round the world trip' to see Dorothy. They just cancelled their travels, and moved right in to look after her, just around the time Peter was going off to University.

Of that time Peter says he felt only a cold numbness, that it is hard to disentangle the events and deterioration up to the revelation, at seventeen, when Dorothy told him she thought she had only a few months to live. He thinks his father's death made him a dysfunctional teenager and that his mother's illness clearly caused him further problems, making it hard to separate the two events in his life. Peter says it helped to run away again, this time to University because the worst part for him was watching the slow relentless deterioration and not being strong enough to really help.

Dorothy lived three more years. It meant the world to her that her illness had not prevented her only son from going to University, for that she could not have borne. When he did not come home as often as some of us felt he should, she remained utterly loyal to him, outwardly rejoicing that he was getting on with his life, for this to her was by far and away her greatest wish.

When he brought girl friends home to meet her, this delighted her even though she would quietly tell me, after their departure, whether or not she felt them suitable for Peter. His infrequent visits brought criticism from some family members, who were unable to grasp what I had come to realise, that it would have distressed Dorothy far more if he had come home too often.

Peter was approaching the end of his degree with finals coming up when Dorothy's condition worsened and home care became no longer viable. Her doctor wanted to admit her to a Hospice in a nearby town and she put up no resistance, on one condition. Peter was not to be told.

She had thought it through she told us and would write him a note, saying she was going into hospital for some treatment. I refused to comply with this and gently, but firmly helped her see that this was in no way fair to Peter. He must know the situation so that he could decide what action to take. I still remember her resolve despite her extreme weakness and it was only when her courteous, old-fashioned doctor agreed with me that she relented.

Peter came immediately to the Hospice and stayed by his mother's side through the night until she slipped peacefully away in the early hours.

In the ensuing years, Peter moved to London and after further training became an asset to the firms he worked with. He visited us on occasion and we visited him and he appeared to be enjoying life, with a stream of attractive girl friends.

Though I had concerns from time to time at the number of young women's hearts Peter seemed to be scattering in his wake, it was only in 1997 that it really hit me that perhaps there was something pathological about this behaviour. It was in the summer of that year when he called at our home unexpectedly and found me alone, that he visibly showed his emotions disclosing potentially serious, unresolved grief.

In listening to him that day I began to see how grief and guilt were emotionally holding him in the past and preventing him from investing himself fully in the present or a future.

Much as I wanted to help him, I knew that I was not the right person to take on a counselling role for all sorts of reasons, not the least that I had made lots of mistakes in our relationship in the past, but more importantly at that time I was attempting to support the most recent of his wounded lovers. I was somewhat surprised that he put up no objection to my suggestion that I felt he should seek counselling, for it is not something men easily agree to.

For the first time, as he drove away from our home, I felt his pain as I had never felt it before. Peter may have had his own home at a very early age and the finance and freedom to travel wherever his fancy took him, unlike our own sons, but at what personal price? Was there anyone out there who would know he was missing if he didn't turn up for a few weeks or months?

Peter thinks he made some progress in at least understanding his problems while attending counselling sessions. He came to realise that his experience had impacted on most of his relationships, up to the point where his partner became pregnant when he felt and enjoyed the love and responsibility of that relationship.

He is now married with three lovely children and says he started fixing his problems after the birth of his daughter in 1999. Watching him with his little ones at bath-time during our last visit, I couldn't help but think how his mother and father would have been so proud and said so, feeling confident that he had moved on from all that grief and guilt of times past.

★ ★ ★

More than twenty years on I am much the wiser and calmer and so much of that I have gained from young people. I have learnt that above all else, we must keep open our lines of communication with them; not in a reactive carping way, as I was with Peter, or by patronising, but in a calm, reasoned and exploratory way. We must allow them to be heard. We will not always like what they are doing, yet we must always let them know we still love them.

When allowed, even children from a very young age can play their part in a family. At times of adversity they should not be viewed as a burden, but as a resource, for they are sensitive to what is going on around them and can comfort in the most unexpected ways, like the breakfast of scrambled eggs made by Mark after his mother had died, or the small child climbing onto Grandma's knee when she is crying.

There were so many ways that our own sons got us through these family losses, none more so than the sheer normality of hearing their shared laughter when interacting with Peter, or Pauline's children.

We cannot not communicate with children. This does sound pedantic but was the title of a training day I attended which delivered a strong theme of the importance of communicating with children, especially about serious sickness in the family or among close friends. Never more so than when a person is dying.

We need first to accept that it is never easy, but there are several publications now to guide us in helping children during these times and Cancerbackup is one such source. (See Appendix Two).

Research has shown that many adults have faced problems in relationships, through loss of a loved one during their childhood or as a young adult. How much wiser we can all be with the benefit of hindsight and increased knowledge and understanding.

For anyone who may be wishing they had done it better in the past, please don't punish yourself. Whatever you did or did not do, if at the time you did it with the child's best interest at heart as Dorothy did, then forgive yourself, for guilt keeps you inside yourself and outside life where you belong. I believe in a strange way, quite unrecognised at the time, that these experiences were part of my training ground for taking on the role of Macmillan Nurse, particularly in relation to the exposure to young adults as survivors of loss. Can any parent imagine a worse scenario than where their young adult son or daughter on the brink of life itself, is struck down with a life-threatening illness? I met with Leila, David and Louise during my first year as a Macmillan Nurse.

# *Chapter Four*

## Young Hopefuls : 1987-9

*I have a dream. Please help me to realise it.*
*Archbishop Tutu.*

At eighteen years of age, Leila was found to have a bone tumour in her leg necessitating an amputation. She had been to University where she had excelled and became an idealist and a leader. I first met her in hospital when, at the age of twenty-two, the cancer had come back this time in her lungs. When there was no response to treatment, she asked to go home where she could be cared for by her mother and boyfriend.

I was assisting in my role as Macmillan Nurse and over a few months, we had become very close. Before she died, she gave me a small pearl of a lesson. The headteacher of a local school had heard about my past successes at creative writing and had invited me in to talk to his 6th form English group. Though I had spoken publicly on many occasions about cancer and Macmillan nursing, even to groups of six-formers, I had never before spoken of my writing. I felt strangely nervous and anxious and wished I had never agreed to do it. On the appointed day, I called to see Leila on my way to the school. When she asked me where I was going next, I told her and also how nervous I was feeling. "Just tell them and you'll be fine," she said.

"Tell them?" I checked, surprised at her suggestion.

"That you're nervous." She smiled. "That way, they'll be on your side from the start."

And so I did and so they were. She had been absolutely right.

Leila, like Ellie knew that she was going to die, sooner rather than later. Within the limitations of their disease, both of these young women summoned amazing courage to do what was important to them and in each case, it was with others in mind.

Leila's biggest disability, was not as you may think that she had only one leg, but rather the breathlessness brought about by the spread of the cancer to her lungs. It necessitated her being cared for in an upright position on a bed in their living room. Just changing position with assistance left her struggling for breath. Yet I never remember a time when she didn't greet me with a smile.

Despite this debility, a few days before she died, Leila persuaded her boyfriend to order a taxi and accompany her to a certain shop in town from where she selected a gift for her father's coming birthday. If asked, I would have refuted the slightest chance of this being possible.

I would like to think that when facing my death I can find this sort of courage. I think I would settle for just half as much! I believe that courage is more easily summoned when one can feel some control of a situation. Ellie and Leila both had that; my friend Roma did not. I refer to the control that goes with having information about one's situation; in this case, their destiny.

Dreams and aspirations are usually at a peak in young adulthood. You would be forgiven for thinking that a young person's dreams are swept away on learning that their disease has become untreatable, that they would lose all sense of control. On the contrary, after the initial reactions, actually knowing what is facing them commonly gives them back control. I have seen it so often.

A different kind of courage seems to be needed for those young people with haematological cancers eminently treatable, increasingly curable, yet clouded in uncertainty and setbacks often for years. This demands a tireless tenacity from them and a sure steadfastness from their family and friends.

I want to allow you a glimpse into the lives of three such individuals along with those closest to them, whose worlds were turned upside down when they came face to face with Hodgkin's Lymphoma. A lymphoma is a malignant proliferation of the lymphoid system where treatment and prognosis depend on the extent of the disease at the time of diagnosis. Chemotherapy and Radiotherapy are most often used, as lymphomas differ from solid tumours in that surgical removal is not an option.

With Hodgkin's Lymphoma, swift eradication is not a reality. Careful unfolding of the truth about likely length of treatment is crucial, hence skilled communication is something at which most Haematologists excel, often over and above the level of their colleagues in other specialties.

David was twenty-two when he became unwell and tests revealed that he had this form of cancer. I still remember the first time I met him. He had come to the hospital straight from his workplace and was still in his motor mechanic's boiler suit. I was struck by his good looks. His girl friend was with him and they were both in shock.

"There must be some kind of mistake," he kept saying.

How much I would have given at that time to agree with him that there had been a mistake; that it had all been some kind of bad dream. Instead, I had been asked to give David an insight into the disease, to prepare him for what lay ahead. Nowadays, with such information at the touch of a computer mouse, most patients like to keep abreast of their disease and treatment. At that time, we used to issue written information to back up whatever we gave them verbally.

David and his girl friend then wanted to know what I could do for them. So I told them about my role. I explained that I worked as a specialist nurse with individuals affected by cancer, and their families. I told them that while I worked very closely with other members of the team involved in David's care, I was also peripatetic in that I didn't have responsibility for all the other patients on the ward, in the clinic or on the district. This way, I had flexibility over how I managed my time, consequently more time for listening, for exploring feelings, for considering ways of overcoming difficulties, and when necessary, for counselling. I explained the special training Macmillan Nurses have in the management of pain and other symptoms, enabling us to liaise and discuss these areas of care with the patient's doctor. I used to arrange to meet up with

David as he came into hospital, either to attend clinic or for his chemo session. Sometimes, his girl friend would be with him. Whenever possible, he would come at the end of a day's work, striving for normality. He had rough times, when the treatment had to be extended, but mostly coped with whatever was thrown at him. He coped with the loss of his hair which I remember all fell out while he was on holiday abroad with his girl friend. He coped with a burn on his arm from a leaked cytotoxic, and with staying away from pubs to avoid infection over New Year when his blood count fell. When Macmillan were making a video, he agreed to be interviewed and starred superbly, answering all questions as if primed. He had a personal meeting with HRH The Prince of Wales and became something of a celebrity when his photo appeared in the local press.

Then everything came tumbling down. After years of treatment and yet more treatment, the disease still persisted. He felt everything was against him and that it was time to give up. His last chance was to undergo more treatment, of a different kind, far from home in a National Centre, with no guarantee of success. He was at his very lowest ebb and facing his most difficult decision.

*A Day to Remember 2004*

I was walking with Brian through our market place one Sunday morning on one of those bright, sunny, good-to-be-alive days, when a young man with a small boy at his side stepped in front of me. "Hi," he greeted us, stopping in his tracks and smiling broadly.

"David!" We hugged each other then I bent down to the child.

"This is my son, Jack," he said with so much pride.

"Hello Jack." Before me was a miniature of his father with the very same blue eyes. "I'm Clare, a friend of your daddy's."

"A very good friend," David exclaimed.  My heart swelled and the good-to-be-alive day was transformed into something quite momentous. Eight years on from diagnosis, David had been given the all clear. He told me he felt very honoured that he had come out OK especially after years of treatment when he had witnessed much death and illness in his many spells in hospital.

When asked, he told me that some doctors and staff could have been more tactful towards him. With hindsight, he says he could have been more helpful towards them. He also says he should have tried to understand what his family were going through.

I think that is one very balanced outlook and I rejoice along with all those who know David, along with his wife and two children, for the living witness that he is to himself and to modern medicine.

★  ★  ★

During those years a sick-looking young man was admitted, who I shall call Philip. He was twenty-seven and husband of one of our nurses. They had a small daughter and another child was on the way. His mother too, was a member of staff, and readers may know that hospitals are a bit like families. When one of its members faces adversity, a whole wave of concern and sympathy builds up, like a great protective wall. Philip's wife was strong and so positive that I don't know that she ever leaned on that wall, but perhaps knowing it was there was enough for her.

From the beginning Philip didn't want to see a Macmillan Nurse and, respecting this, I only recall brief moments spent with him. There was an awareness, that for him this disease was like a huge boulder, which had knocked him completely off course. His wife has told me, 'He was never the same person – his personality changed – at times he talked of suicide, which was unbelievably hard. This despite being told he had 98% chance of cure.'

I do not know who it was who first said 'It is not what happens to us in life that matters, but what we do with what happens to us.' I would like to add three little words so that it reads 'It is not what happens to us in life that matters, but what we *are able to* do with what happens to us'.

The going was very rough for both Philip and his wife. When she had to undergo a Caesarean Section, she recalls feeling glad that it fitted well between his chemo sessions. Inevitably, the safe arrival of their healthy son was overshadowed by Philip's disease. Tragically, Philip died in less than one year from the start of his illness. His wife is a remarkable living witness for any survivor of such a loss. After her husband's death, there were times of terrible sadness, overwhelming loss and great barrenness, yet never hopelessness. She set herself very high expectations, resolving from early days that once her children were old enough, she wanted to do cancer nursing. We have kept in touch and meet from time to time. As I write, her children are nine and ten and with her own and her family's support seem to be doing really well. As they have grown, she has increased her working hours, and has pursued her career both clinically and academically. She is a credit to our profession and now has a ward sister's post in a regional cancer centre.

She tells me her experience has made her 'live for the day more'. It has made her stronger, a feeling that having coped with such a great loss, she can cope with anything now. She also says that it has made her a better nurse and more aware of the impact of cancer on a whole family.

You are a courageous and principled young woman. I hold you in high esteem. I only urge you and others like you, in your drive to serve others best, remember also to be kind to yourself.

Louise was only nineteen when she was told she had cancer. I still remember her small, frightened face that first day when I met her in the double side-room of a medical ward. "I'm scared," she whispered between tears. "But I'll beat it." Then she groaned. "But my hair!" She gripped my hand. "Why me anyway?"

I have many memories of Louise, mostly of marvelling at the way this slip of a girl, grew into a fine young woman during those early months of treatment. The somewhat timid person became an assertive, independent one, which I suspect may have been hard for her mother at that time, for much as she would want that for her daughter, like most mothers, it also raises feelings of letting go and loss. Add that to the trauma associated with a life-threatening illness and such a potent concoction of emotions is difficult to imagine.

Louise coped with her hair loss by having an amazing,

authentic looking wig of long, dark hair that looked stunning against her pale skin. She too was generous in agreeing to appear in the same Macmillan video as David.

During those years when the role of the Macmillan Nurse was changing towards that of a 'cancer nurse specialist for the living', its' association with the terminally ill was still strong. Few referrals came our way unless someone was thought to have a very poor outlook or to be actually facing death. These young people and others with haematological malignancies were the exception and the more so in the area I worked, thanks to an enlightened consultant. So to me, they brought a balance to my workload and a joyful one at that, despite times of great disappointment and anxiety. Their cancer journeys were very different for there was frequently hope for a good outcome, despite difficult and lengthy periods of treatment.

I don't believe it occurred to me at the time, but being accepted into a friendship with these young people, over a period when our own sons were breaking free from parental bondage as it were, was a particularly profound privilege. On reflection, I suspect it greatly reduced my sense of loss during that time of transition.

There is often a downside to the joy of experiencing success, from which we cannot escape. I remember one Christmas Eve, preparing to go off duty, making last minute phone calls to colleagues and families from my office in the hospital, when my pager went off.

"Can you come down to the Clinic?" It was Dr Mack's secretary. "Louise is here and would like to see you."

I was delighted. Some months back, she had moved to a

new job in London, in remission and returning regularly for routine checks. She must have arranged this one to tie up with coming home for Christmas.

My footsteps echoed an emptiness as I made my way along the clinic corridor, for many support staff had already begun their Christmas leave. I found Louise sitting with the secretary in her office.

"It's back," she sobbed, as I went to her.

All the joy of Christmas went from me in that moment while she let me just hold her.

"What am I going to do?" she whispered.

"You're going to send it packing," I urged her. "Just as you did before."

★ ★ ★

For some time, after my change of role with Macmillan, I lost touch with Louise. Then one Christmas, I received a wedding photo, which I have before me as I write this. This bride is very slight with long, dark hair framing a tanned face, dressed in a beautiful white bridal dress. Beside her is her handsome groom, holding her lovingly and protectively. In her letter, Louise tells me he is a single father with a small son and that this is all she had ever dreamed of but never believed possible.

She was twenty-four when she was given the all clear and says it was two more years before she dared believe that she had beaten it. Even to this day, she says she still worries about every ache and pain, fearing it may come back.

Like David, she too recalls that some of the doctors were abrupt, making unnecessarily upsetting remarks. She particularly remembers overhearing one doctor saying to a night nurse 'It's okay to cry – she might die'. This she says spurred her on to prove them wrong! She believes thinking positive is the key to getting through and wants doctors to stop being negative. Lest anyone reading this also feels doctors could do better, I can tell you that many would agree. It is never easy to find the right words at the right time in these situations, especially when one is called upon to be honest. In a world where so much is visual, the ability to listen is vital. The dearth of training in communication skills, listening in particular, needs to be remedied. Before me I have another, more recent photo, of Louise's step-son aged ten holding his new brother at a year old – the outcome of her 'miracle conception'.

There are so *many* others I remember, patients and their loved ones, whose stories are equally inspiring, if only space allowed. Please know, you not only touched my life but the lives of so many who were alongside you on your journey.

*Douglas Macmillan. Born 1884*

It feels timely here to include the story of another young person whose life was turned upside-down by cancer, and yet whose resoluteness, courage and commitment, compelled him to use his experience for the benefit of others. Douglas Macmillan has been described as a David of his time, facing the Goliath of the medical and political establishments. He was not privileged to belong to the Macmillans of either political or publishing fame; but like those families, he came from Scott's Presbyterian stock.

Douglas was born on August 10th 1884 in Castle Cary,

Somerset. Castle Cary was then, as now, a small town which had obtained a market charter from Edward VI in 1468. Situated within easy reach of Wells, Glastonbury and Frome, it nestles between a gentle blending of hill and vale. Douglas grew up in this lively market town dominated by the prosperity of its mills.

He was the fifth son of a fifth son, and also the seventh child of a seventh child. His father, William Macmillan, was a county magistrate and a well-respected member of the local community; his mother, Emily, equally known for her good works. At the age of 13, Douglas attended a Quaker school, one of the first co-eds in the country, indicating a certain amount of liberal thinking in his parents. His academic abilities and leadership qualities were certainly recognised as he finished there as head boy in 1900.

He gained a studentship to Birkbeck College in London and in 1905 he was appointed permanently to the Board of Agriculture and Fisheries and moved to London, where he met and married his first wife.

It was 1911 when his father aged 61, fell seriously ill and died of cancer of the oesophagus. The effect on this 27-year-old civil servant was to lead him to a deep concern and interest in cancer and its consequences on patients and their families.

In fact it was as a direct result of his father's death that Douglas was determined to help other sufferers. Several years later, in a booklet to all Macmillans, he wrote of his father, "He was scarcely past the prime of an intensely active life and had never known illness previously. It was a cruel tragedy during those last months to watch him wasting into weakness. When the end came, being I suppose at an impressionable age, I was more affected than by anything else in my experience. Could nothing be done to prevent such seemingly needless destruction?"

He suggests in the booklet that all Macmillans should consider the invitation to become life members of the National Society of Cancer Relief – now Macmillan Cancer Support – by contributing £10. He says that it was his father's custom on his birthday to distribute gifts to his family and it was with the last such gift to his son that the foundations of the society were laid.

Douglas had no medical background but by using his family and friends he pioneered Macmillan Cancer Support. It existed entirely on the subscriptions of interested individuals and concentrated its efforts on providing information on recognising, preventing and treating cancer to patients, doctors and interested members of the public. In Douglas's own words "I want people to be provided with the latest and best advice for avoiding cancer and for recognising and dealing with it when it exists."

The years leading up to the 1930's depression were a time of great poverty for many and cancer was becoming more understood as a killer disease.

During 1924, Douglas bought a house in Sidcup from where he managed his Society and registered and established it as a benevolent society.

By 1930 the first full time paid member of staff, an appeals officer, was employed. By now Douglas decided he wanted to see 'homes for cancer patients throughout the land where attention will be provided freely or at low cost' and 'panels of nurses who can attend to necessitous patients in their homes'. This vision even before the Welfare State had been conceived! By 1933 the society was providing 278 cancer patients and their families with a small weekly allowance to cover the cost of medicines, dressings and extra food.

From very humble beginnings the perseverance of this man was beginning to bear fruit. Even with this time-consuming involvement Douglas continued with his full time occupation as a civil servant for which he received the M.B.E. in 1944, before retiring the following year at the age of 61 to devote his time to the Society.

The introduction of the National Health Service made some provision for patients with cancer by providing or paying for dressings, drugs, surgical appliances and transport to hospital. But as a Society bulletin stated in 1948 "Legislation however generous and welcome is never likely to cancel out the need for a supplementary and personal service." I believe the same is true to this day.

It was in 1963 when due to his advancing years and ill health, Douglas decided to retire from his 50 years' work for the Society which had by now moved to offices in London and Douglas was succeeded as Chairperson by the Duchess of Roxburghe. The Society's income was then about £250,000 all received from personal donations, subscriptions, legacies and fund raising by local committees of which there were 170 in 1964.

In April 1969 Douglas Macmillan died at his home aged 84 of the disease he had worked so actively to relieve.

By 1975 Macmillan Cancer Support had built and equipped the first of its own cancer care units in Christchurch, Dorset, to provide in-patient and day care for cancer patients. In that same year the first Macmillan nurses were established and in 1980 Macmillan's education programme was begun, to teach doctors, nurses and other allied health professionals the latest techniques of pain control and cancer care.

Douglas Macmillan's legacy to our nation has been one of great magnitude. In this new century Macmillan Cancer Support completed their hundredth building, providing a calm and reassuring atmosphere for treatment and care. At the end of 2006 the 170 local committees of 1964 stood at 514, payments of £8.175 million were given in patient grants helping over 22,000 people living with cancer, who may have lost their jobs or already be on low incomes, to meet extra costs caused by illness, and Macmillan posts numbered 4,155 with 3003 of those being nurses. A long, long way from Douglas's two full time 'Nurse Visitors', appointed in London and York in 1933.

As an independent body Macmillan has the opportunity – and the obligation – to look ahead and consider how its considerable resources and reputation could be used to secure the best services for people affected by cancer, now and in the future.

Macmillan post-holders whether nurses, doctors, social workers or other allied health professionals are all qualified, experienced individuals when appointed. They go on to receive further professional development through Macmillan's Education Programmes, ensuring that patient care is continually improving. Macmillan post-holders are not in the employment of Macmillan Cancer Support, but within the National Health Service where they are best placed in their vital roles in building ever better cancer services. It is Macmillan which makes these posts possible by funding all costs, usually for the first three years. Through working in partnership in this way Macmillan, in ever more innovative ways, continues to make a real difference for people living with cancer, from diagnosis onwards.

Difficulties can lie in the very success of a Macmillan Service, as I discovered, for with that initial funding goes a pledge that the NHS Trust will fund thereafter. So while a community can raise funds for another Macmillan post, with a strapped-for-cash NHS, it may not come about, as I painfully experienced back in the late 1980s.

# Chapter Five

## Teetering on Survival

*The tragedy of life is what dies inside a man while he lives.*

Dr Albert Schweitzer. *1875-1965*

As the New Year dawned in 1989 I lay awake, tormented by thoughts of what the year ahead might bring. I was now four months into my second year alone and knew that I was at the point of exhaustion, both physically and emotionally. What disturbed me most, was how I could keep going on my own, or even worse, *if* I could.

Because the Community Service in our Health District had not seen a Macmillan Service as the best way forward for them, there had been agreement to the appointment of only one nurse based in the hospital, not, it must be said, without concerns from Macmillan who recommended no single nurse service. I was charged with the following objective:

*'To contribute to the total nursing care and management of the terminally ill patient, relatives and carers by offering support and specialised nursing advice to the patient, his/her relatives, carers, health care professionals and others involved in care. To build up a centre of excellence in the specialty.'* No mean feat for one lone soul.

Note the emphasis at that time on 'the terminally ill patient' rather than 'the person with cancer'. It is not difficult to see where the confusion was born around Macmillan Nurses being perceived as 'angels of death'. Thankfully their roles have long since evolved, appropriately, to those of nurses who specialise in cancer care.

On the day of my appointment, I remember going out to celebrate with Brian and the youngest of our three sons, then aged 18, the only one at home at the time. I little realised then, how much this new post would impinge on our family life. My first year in post had been an extremely busy one with more referrals from more areas, totalling 240 patients. As the Service became more widely recognised, so demands increased, resulting either in inability to accept a referral, or a lengthier deferral time.

Where Macmillan involvement continued after patients were discharged from Hospital, GPs and District Nurses from Primary Health Care Teams welcomed such support with increasing enthusiasm. The hospital-based nature of the service helped enormously in bridging the divide that tends to arise between hospital and community.

There has never been any doubt that care for the terminally ill and their families is a fundamental part of all who care for the sick, but hospital staff insisted that their training had not equipped them for this task. Some community staff expressed the same sentiment and began to acknowledge the value of a Nurse Specialist with a concentrated growing expertise in the care of the terminally ill cancer patient. It needs to be remembered this was way back in the 1980s when frontiers in the understanding and management of cancer were moving at a more rapid pace than generalists could hope to be kept abreast. There was recognition that the only way to narrow the gap between patients' needs and ability to meet them was to offer support and teaching to all staff.

Of course I agreed with this and so organised sessions across the District to staff of several disciplines. I hung on in there for that first year, working all hours, in the belief that when the powers-that-be received the Annual Report and saw the way the service was over-stretched, a decision to appoint a second nurse would be taken. I had not however allowed for the bureaucracy of unwieldy organisations and the political to-ing and fro-ing, which gets in the way of service delivery. I was told that this was a difficult time for all Health Districts with tightening of expenditure and demands from many quarters. While there was support for a second nurse, no commitment could be taken that Health District funding would be available in three years, even allowing that Macmillan could presently meet this request. The situation would be kept under review.

I began to feel resentment towards senior nurse management when I was told to prioritise my work and pass patients back to their primary carer, once I had seen them. I had been practising this since taking up the post, whenever and wherever it was possible, too often to the distress of patients and family. Even though from first contact, it was explained to patients that I had been called in to help with a particular problem, inevitably a relationship of trust would develop so that when their situation resolved and I told them I would not be arranging to see them again, there would be expressions of great disappointment, along with a real sense of abandonment, however good their primary carers were. As you may imagine, for any Macmillan Nurse, this could be deeply troubling and painful, for these were people already vulnerable and here I was inflicting further loss.

Professionally, I rationalised that their needs would and could now be met by their main carers, and continuing ongoing support with them would mean denying someone else input from the Macmillan Service. I did realise my limitations and yet was faced with the awful dilemma, in the absence of increased resources, of how to spread myself even thinner and survive. I really did try to be wise. On reflection, I believe I was foolish however in one respect, at least.

When I came into post the service was re-launched. Senior Management had cards printed giving my name and contact details, including my home phone number. This was considered part of the tactics of good sales promotion of a service we all wanted to succeed. Had I considered the consequences however, I would have opposed it as home now became an extension of my work place. I never minded the phone calls for advice, in fact I welcomed them as I had come to know the difference that accuracy or fine-tuning of medication could make to a patient's comfort or a dignified death, but some situations were particularly complex and beyond my experience. For those I had identified two resource links, one a Consultant in Palliative Care at an excellent teaching Hospice in a neighbouring town, another an Oncology Consultant with whom I had worked closely.

When I did make it home after a long day's work, I

always had paperwork to do; either writing up patient notes, preparing teaching material or collecting statistics for reports. This was not optional for the sustainability of the service. I simply had to keep going. Macmillan Nursing had become a way of life and there was little time for anything else. Brian would gently chide me to unwind and relax, and though I wanted to, I simply could not find the time.

★ ★ ★

My chosen field of nursing constantly exposes me to the emotional pain of others. Much as miners cannot avoid the dust of the substance they excavate, so Macmillan Nurses and others working in the same sphere cannot be shielded from the hurt and grief of those for whom they care.

Wholeness in health embraces body, mind and spirit. When you become physically exhausted, you become mentally and spiritually fatigued, and emotionally vulnerable.

Knowing this in your head does not in itself protect you, as I learnt to my cost. I had recently become involved in the care of a seven-year-old boy with cancer. Most of his care up to then had been in hospital in the Regional Children's Centre, with an outreach nurse making the home visits. When the disease persisted after all possible treatment was finally exhausted his parents brought him home to die, which was when the Primary Health Care Team asked me in to help.

He was a brave little boy who spoke about seeing his Gran when he went to heaven. This in itself was tough enough, but his parents were bereft and consoling them was even tougher.

Sometimes in such situations, the very closest and loving of relationships can become acrimonious, when all hope of survival fades and death comes rushing onwards with the speed of an express train. So it was for this family. The parents were at different places on their tragic journey, so that when one managed to raise a smile, he was accused by the other of being unfeeling, uncaring. The visiting GP and district nurse found the situation unfathomable, which demanded the very keenest of skills in support for them all.

Attending funerals can become an occupational hazard for Macmillan Nurses and each one should be very carefully considered. Why am I going? Sometimes the reason is very clear; it can be for the bereaved family who have come to see you as one of them, or for yourself when you have become very attached to the deceased and need to be there to say your goodbyes. It should never be simply because people expect it of you. Then, a note to the bereaved telling them you are not able to attend but that you will be thinking of them, I believe to be very acceptable.

My reason for going to this small boy's funeral was clear to me. It was a gesture of respect to his parents who had bared themselves to me during those final weeks. I felt that by being there, I would be a silent witness to their courage in coming together in harmony, with renewed love for each other before the death of their child.

I stayed towards the back of the church, behind a pillar, feeling a need for privacy, both for myself and for the close family circle and friends, in what I consider, this very public tradition. I stood as others did as the small coffin was carried in followed by family mourners. It was a beautiful service if such a thing can be said, with meaningful prayers and readings. As it began to draw to a close, the organ struck up very softly to the tune of 'All Things Bright and Beautiful.'

I hugged myself for I had suddenly become very cold. I heard the congregation get to their feet, but I couldn't join them for a weakness had come over me. I was unable to help myself up. It was as if an enormous wave had engulfed me so that I couldn't even get my breath. My head fell forward, part buried in my hands. I was shaking, silent sobs racking my body. I felt afraid for I could not control myself. I had never felt like this before; never. I really don't know how long it lasted, but it seemed forever. The singing ended, then I heard the voice of the priest as if somewhere far distant. I kept my head down until the sound of retreating footsteps fell silent and the last voice faded away. Slowly, when I was able, I raised my head to an empty church. I felt completely empty, drained and lifeless and began to realise that I had slipped out of my Macmillan role and into the role of a mother, a mother who has lost her child.

★  ★  ★

I am a very introspective person and never more so than in the early hours of the morning, while the rest of the world sleeps. They are the worst times, when one's mind will not be stilled, when fears are heightened, when reason seems out of grasp, when more than anything else one yearns for the oblivion of sleep.

Strangely, though my work was deluged in others' loss and awash with sadness, it was seldom this that disturbed me and kept me awake. Usually I knew that by being there in my privileged role as Macmillan Nurse, I had relieved some distress. Whether that had been physical, psychological, social, sexual or spiritual, whether it had been through direct contact with the patient or a loved one, or through encouraging or empowering a member of the health care team, generally I knew that between us we had made things as good as they could be under the circumstances. They are the rewards and believe me, they are priceless. What mostly kept me awake was the sheer enormity of the workload. To give you some idea, I was trying to do then what is now being done by three Macmillan Nurses, plus a Haematology Nurse Specialist, a Lung Nurse Specialist and a Breast Care Nurse. Speaking with one of them recently, I understand that the battle with workload and time continues. Neither was there a local hospice at that time. This only opened in the September of 1989, after I had been in post alone for two years.

As I lay awake in the early hours of that New Year's Day, I was racked with anxiety and remorse and almost worse, with tiny seeds of resentment. I was anxious about my exhaustion and whether I could carry on single-handed in the face of so much work. Expectations had been raised, trust had been won, pain had been mastered, new knowledge gained all resulting in better patient care. Macmillan was now high profile in our District, making a difference to the lives of those with cancer.

Yet I had an urge to become invisible, for my exhaustion was such that I felt anxious whenever I cleared my ansaphone of more and more new referrals. With an already full diary of appointments, when could I possibly see new patients, and for how much longer on my own?

The remorse I felt was about my schizoid-like behaviour. I had heard talk of people, usually children, being 'street angel, house devil' and I feared I had become just that. To my colleagues, patients and their families I believe I was approachable, warm, kind and considerate, compassionate, patient with their foibles, and strong. To my family, who I loved most dearly, quite unintentionally I had become distant, impatient and at times, harsh. I wept tears of self-reproach for this was really not how I wanted to be. I have never found it easy to surrender myself in all my vulnerability, and on reflection I must have hidden under the prickly coat of a hedgehog instead of admitting to them my terrible tiredness. During such times of exhaustion-induced stress, or burnout, my husband and sons have gone on loving me unconditionally. They have been the sunshine in my shadows; something I can never forget and know I have not always deserved.

Seeds of resentment, like the fluffy heads of dandelions had begun to blow in my face. In the light of day, I could whack them away for I knew them to be damaging, self-destructive. In the darkness, like mushrooms they will sprout and take hold. I felt resentment towards Macmillan for allowing a single nurse appointment, even while knowing it was the only way in this District that they could ever hope to start.

I resented their lack of support after appointment, their nationwide advertising which I knew to be necessary for their fund-raising, while this only generated more and more work and I also resented their calls on my time to receive cheques on their behalf. I think most of all, petty though it may seem now, I resented their failure even to acknowledge my first Annual Report.

I also felt resentment towards the decision-makers in my Health District for their unwillingness to find funds for a second Macmillan Nurse. Finally, I resented those few health professionals who would not seek help or advice to better their patients' care, and to the other few who would side-step their responsibility and refer anyone with a diagnosis of cancer.

I don't actually recall praying during that time which indicates to me how low I must have been. Mercifully at some point I called a halt. I would not be pulled down, spoiled by resentment. I would find the energy and the time to do something about it.

So enough of that for now; let me return to the real heart of my work as a Macmillan Nurse and share the stories of some of the women I was privileged to  walk alongside, probably quite ordinary women, who became extra ordinary when faced with adversity.

# *Chapter Six*

## Women of Substance : 1987-92

> *As we let our own light shine, we unconsciously give others permission to do the same.*
>
> Marianne Williamson.

It is more than fifteen years since Sally died yet whenever I see a rainbow I think about her, and remember her rainbow.

We only came together through her advanced cancer, yet over a few months, a deep and special relationship developed between us. From our very first meeting I felt totally at ease with her, a feeling I believe that was mutual.

"I have enjoyed your visit," she told me as I got up to leave. "Immensely," she added, smiling. "When will you come again?"

In appearance, Sally was like fine porcelain, delicate and needing to be cherished, yet robust in spirit. To her family, she was a wife, a mother, a daughter and a sister. They all wanted her well again so that life could return to normal.

In those early visits, she was hopeful that following recent surgery there would be some improvement. She admired and trusted her surgeon whose skills were indeed renowned. Miracles, sadly, were not within his power.

When the moment felt right to ask Sally how she saw the future, she responded to my gentle probing by speaking of her dying and sharing her fears. Always, I left her in control of the pace of such discussions, respecting her faith which brought her great strength and comfort.

Sometimes she would share areas of her life not directly related to her condition, but with a child-like sparkle and sense of fun that were a joy to behold. I treasured such moments of intimacy and thought how much I would have loved to have known her earlier for I believe we would have been good friends. I think that was how Sally saw it too and that makes me very happy.

Her greatest struggle was having sufficient intake of food to sustain her and avoid further weight loss. Even without weighing scales, it wasn't long before she became aware that all items from her lovely, classic wardrobe, hung loosely on her. Yet always, she took great effort to present herself well, layering and co-ordinating garments and accessories and taking time with her hair and make-up.

"I so want to look well for my family," she would tell me.

Her family were the main focus of her life. Her eldest son was an officer in the army and away, while her daughter and younger son, still in education, were closer at hand.

Her husband worked locally. As with all families there

were anxieties over one thing or another, and differences of opinion, all I suspect, exacerbated by Sally's condition. When she shared these issues with me, she would go to enormous lengths dissecting them and exploring different ways of approach to achieve the best result. Such discussions fell comfortably within the boundaries of my role as Macmillan Nurse, as much as those around her illness and the future. Sally needed, as I believe most sick people do, to retain her role in the family, for even while physically weakening, her mind remained strong and intact.

During one of my visits, she wanted to show me her new kitchen. She had been resting upstairs and as I assisted her down the elegant staircase, I could hear someone moving about in the kitchen, from where an aroma of herbs was drifting. Her eldest son was home and was cooking dinner. She smiled at him appreciatively. I made remarks about the new kitchen and his chivalrous preparation of food. Then this very personable young man, sensitive to his mother's frailty, gently ushered us towards the door. "Come along now," he said. "Out of my kitchen please."

Sally's hand in mine gripped tightly and the look she gave me, spoke volumes. Once seated in the lounge, she spoke. "It used to be my kitchen." Her voice was filled with such sorrow that for a few moments I was choked and said nothing. Yet there was no discomfort in the ensuing silence. Any words would have been banal. Recognition of losing ground, of the nearness of death, can come in so many different ways. For Sally, this was one.

Recalling it now, brings to mind the importance for those whose time is short, to feel they still have a role to play. I believe this to be as true for the elderly as for the terminally ill. Carers and close family and friends need to be aware of the significance of this. The sick and the elderly should be allowed and at times encouraged to retain their role among us, even though the boundaries of that role will by necessity become fluid, like a tide ebbing and flowing. Often, our sick and elderly come to feel that they are useless, or a burden, that their lives have become meaningless. At such times we need to listen to their feelings, not dismissing them but acknowledging regretfully that they have them. Then, with sensitivity and foresight, let the person know how much they are valued as friend, family or part of our community. Tell them it is they who provide us with an opportunity to care, which in turn helps us to grow in humanity. It is they who allow for us a time to be still, away from the fast track of life, to learn from them and often, through trying to feel the depth of their pain, to sense again the sheer joy of each new day; of 'the present'.

When one steps into the shadows of another's sickness or old age, one can come to feel the sunshine in a way one may never have felt it before. It may even be possible to see a rainbow that is yours alone. I believe to this day, that Sally sent me a rainbow.

I was with her that last evening before she died, there in her bedroom with its lovely view over the fields and beyond to the woods. In the week leading up to her death, she had become increasingly translucent, as if a great peace had taken residence within her. Yet in her few whispered words, I sensed there still remained concern for her family.

I remember telling her that she had done everything

possible for them, that though they would miss her terribly, they would survive and that one-day, they would be fine again. As I drove away, the evening shadows were lengthening and though the world was beautiful, I felt a heaviness of spirit, knowing that I too would miss Sally.

When morning came and with it the expected 'phone call, along with the sadness I felt a sense of thanksgiving, that I had known her, if only for a short time. My sighting of a rainbow came as I sat at traffic lights on my way home from work. It seemed to speak to me, of the wonder of nature and of an existence beyond our own. It was of particular brilliance and sharpness and yet no one else I spoke to had seen it. In my mind's eye, it came to me several times that week, and for me it will always be Sally's rainbow.

Sally's husband told me recently me that he and their children are fine and while never forgetting her, have accepted their great loss and are all doing well.

Eileen, unlike Sally, lived for many years after her first encounter with cancer. She was an inspiring woman who handled her life and her cancer in her own unique way. I met her some years after her first confrontation with the disease. At the time, she was about to start treatment for her lungs, a new and somewhat un-orthodox method which involved her travelling some distance.

"I'll have everything they can give me," she told me, "if it helps me function better."

A few years on, she agreed to come along to the local Cancer Support Group to share her story. "So long as you don't expect me to join," she said. "I'm too busy getting on with life to want to stop off and delve back into the problem of my illness."

No such expectations should ever be made of people. What is important is to provide information of what is available, so allowing the person to make his or her own choice. The group environment can be enormously supportive to some, while to others it holds nothing.

So Eileen came along to the group as guest speaker. For a whole hour, she held centre stage while everyone sat spellbound, listening to her every word.

"I am an intolerant person," she told them, "so I cope because I don't tolerate disease. I let these doctors know that I am a human person, not just a number. Don't I Clare?" She turned to me for confirmation.

"You certainly do," I endorsed, recalling clinic appointments when she'd done just that, though not in so many words. She was never rude, but always direct in her challenging questioning. I well remember one rather shy consultant who was escaping the consulting room, even while speaking, by backing almost stealthily towards the door.

"Don't go yet," Eileen said with all her inimitable charm. "I've things to ask."

A momentary cringe swept the doctor's face, quickly replaced by a half smile of surrender. "If you can relax," Eileen was now saying to the group, "then you can get over to them how you feel. I don't just settle for their spiel and let them go. I believe in making my mark." There followed a ripple of approval and laughter. "And another thing; it is really good to take someone with you. You see, when the news isn't good, your mind goes blank and you hear nothing more. So what *you* don't hear, the person with you will."

How right she was. Thankfully, more and more doctors are suggesting that patients be accompanied, though this can immediately imply that what they have to tell you is going to be bad or serious, which of course may not be so. I believe it should be standard practice from the time that first investigations are carried out, when serious findings are suspected. As health professionals increasingly come to realise the value of listening to patients, so sensitivity in care improves.

"So I've just got on with my life," Eileen went on, "being a wife and mother, holidays abroad, my work and my singing."

"What about during times of treatment?" one young member asked.

"Oh yes!" She smiled. "Being subject to chemotherapy does prevent you getting on with your life." She paused briefly before going on. "You can get really down, and anti-social and moody."

There were murmured agreements and heads nodding. "That's when it gets tricky for the partner," one husband-carer said. "It knocks you off track and you don't know how to be."

Eileen nodded agreement. She was an attractive woman, who had come to know the colours and clothes to wear to look her best. She was looking particularly good that evening, with such radiance and animation, that it was difficult to accept that she had lung secondaries for which she was about to have more radiotherapy treatment. "You see," she said, almost mischievously, "we women can give vent to our feelings. Most men can't, so don't." Then on a more serious note, "But chemotherapy can leave you with no energy, even to walk around. You get washed and dressed and you're done." She paused, as if considering before going on.

"Now that is when I get really frustrated. Then another day, even if I only clean out the breadbin, I feel I have achieved something. When I have a really bad day, I just write it off and hope the next will be better. When it isn't, I get angry. Sometimes it can be so awful that I say to my husband, 'I wanna wake up dead tomorrow.' And he says 'you can't' so I get on with it." She laughed. "It can make life hell for my husband, who is the reason I am here today." She paused, looked around and grinned. "Then when the treatment's over and I'm let loose, I make the most of it until they nab me again."

Then Eileen told the story of the time one consultant said he'd like to see her the following week. "I can't," she'd told him. "I have another appointment." She raised her arched eyebrows. "With the Queen." Sure enough, she was due to attend the Buckingham Palace Garden Party and nothing would stop her. She went on to tell the group how after her last chemotherapy, she had been to Italy with her husband; how she had just returned from Portugal with the Folk Choir, where she had prayed at a shrine to Our Lady and returned home with new courage and determination to face this next lot of treatment.

Someone asked if she accepted her cancer. "I do not." She looked at me. "Clare'll tell you. I moan like hell. It frustrates me to the point of tearing my hair out."

"Have you never lost your hair?" asked Louise, sitting there in one of her lovely wigs.

"No. But if I do I've thought of having a completely shaved do, where they paint your head like I've seen on television. Then I'd be right up to the minute. Don't you think?"

Everyone laughed for nothing seemed less likely, than a shaved, painted head on this elegantly dressed woman before them.

"Tell them about your treats," I prompted.

"Oh I pamper myself with chocolate, cream cakes, meal out, hair do. I feel I deserve it, so I have it." Her real spirit was showing through and again there was laughter.

"I don't think you should feel guilty about anything, if it helps you cope. When I'm low, I discuss my problems with my friends, but I'm always careful not to bore them, in case I lose them. All my friends are wonderful," she continued. "They all back me to the hilt and not one has left me since I started all of this eleven years ago." She paused to take a drink.

"One friend particularly taught me a lot. You see I was only thirty eight with a very young family when I was first told. After the surgery, it stopped me doing some things. I could no longer do all I wanted to with the children. I think I began to feel a bit sorry for myself. Then I thought about this friend with multiple schlerosis, who never complains, so I thought I'd better not either." She said it so matter-of-factly. "I was mobile, she wasn't. Without knowing it she is a real boost to me, a little rock. So I told myself to get on with it." Again she smiled. "And I have. Life is for living! My husband and I have worked together to make the most of our life. But the big E for effort has to come from within."

She looked towards where I was sitting with my colleague Hazel and smiled broadly. "But it's also thanks to the Macmillan nurses, who act as a buffer. And to my excellent G.P., who always works so hard for me. When I consider all the love given to me," her eyes swept the room, "and the love I have for my husband, family and friends; I know they need me as much as I need them." She said all this without faltering, which I know I couldn't have done.

"That love provides me with a sense of purpose. Therefore I shall pursue my goal to the end."

And so she did. Eileen chose to go into the local hospice from where she held court when able, and where her appearance, her dignity and her unique spirit were maintained, right up to the time of her death, with the family she loved so dearly, at her side.

Sally and Eileen, while coming from quite different backgrounds, could both be described as middle class, some would say privileged. In materialistic terms this is true in that they both had their own homes, took overseas holidays and had elegant wardrobes. It is none of those things however, which place them in my category of 'women of substance'. Rather it was their spirit towards life and how they coped with what happened to them. It is my experience this has nothing to do with materialistic wealth. I believe Kath's story will illustrate this.

When I was approached by Macmillan's Press Office, and

asked if I could identify a young woman who would be willing to tell her story to a national women's magazine, I immediately thought of Kath. There were two reasons for this; the first that they wanted to focus on the role of a Macmillan Nurse with a patient *living* with cancer; the second because Kath would be seen by readers as a very ordinary woman with whom they could easily identify. I felt her gutsy and extraordinary spirit would do so much to encourage others. I was not prepared for some of the things she said about me to the feature writer and so have to admit to plain embarrassment on that front, though probably the staff in the Macmillan Press Office were delighted! More importantly to me, Kath was so pleased when the feature was published including photographs of her and me together, in the woods outside her home.

At the time, she was thirty eight and in five years since her cancer diagnosis, had undergone five operations, two courses of chemotherapy, and intensive radiotherapy. Her husband worked as a gamekeeper on an estate, where much was expected of him, for very little remuneration. They had three teenage sons and all lived together in a house on the edge of the estate.

Finance was an on-going struggle, yet Kath met all such difficulties with a resourcefulness and sense of humour, unmatched in my experience. She was the first person I had ever known who one might be persuaded, *could* make a silk purse out of a sow's ear! She had an eagle eye for a bargain and a flair for home making. Over and above all that, she had guts and would set herself targets which to most women would seem crazily unrealistic; yet during the time I knew her, she achieved every one.

Her most persistent problem was pain and numbness in one arm, due either to residual disease or scarring from treatment. While we were able to alleviate this with drugs, she found the side effects of the drugs intolerable and was not easily persuaded to consider other measures such as nerve blocks.

Despite this handicap, Kath stripped and redecorated their cottage throughout, with only minimal and occasional help, never failing to have a wholesome and hot meal ready for her men folk when they returned from work or school. She also played her part in the rearing of pups when new litters came along; even when that meant staying up half the night.

She always stopped everything to make a welcoming mug of coffee whenever she heard my car, as she did the morning I was taking out the magazine containing her story. I was disappointed with it for it wasn't as much *her* story as mine. 'She's my miracle worker' read the title quoting Kath. I felt embarrassed that they had got it wrong, for it was she, not I, who was the real miracle worker.

Even when times got much harder, she kept right on, always cheerful, never complaining, but doing her very best for her family. I doubt there was ever a dull moment in that home, for Kath was full of life and had the ability to summon up the most amazing energy, vigour and sense of fun. There was no way one was allowed to feel sorry for her and many of my memories are of shared laughter at her outrageous tales.

Her relationship with her husband could at best be described as volatile as she asked a lot of herself and expected the same from him. I remember her telling the feature writer, 'We've had our ups and downs and some really tough moments. But we're still together.' That had been then, before she finally moved out, she and her youngest son who was still at school, and their faithful old dog.

"I need some peace for the time I have left," she told me with no hint of bitterness. "There's a place in town that social have found for me. It's not much now but I'll make something of it."

And she did. In a matter of weeks, with the help of a small grant from Macmillan, she transformed a dark, uninspiring flat into something resembling a mews apartment. She scanned the local free paper for bargains; she had a friend accompany her to car-boot sales and whenever she had the time and was able, she sewed. The entrance was through a cluttered, small back yard, which once cleared, she transformed with pots of flowering plants.

It was from this haven of peace she created, that in time Kath was able to plan for the future, while still living each day to its full. She arranged for good and trusted friends to be named guardians to her youngest son, but only after talking it through with him first, and his two older brothers, who remained close while showing much of their mother's gusto in setting up homes independently. As time went by, and her illness progressed, she agreed to meet staff from the local hospice and began to attend Day Care.

It seems only fitting that in bringing her story to a close, I let Kath have the last words. The following is a letter she left me, quite the most precious gift I could have wished for as a Macmillan Nurse.

*Dear Clare,*

*Don't worry this is not going to be a morbid letter, just one of many thanks for being a special friend. This was to last for seven years. I could never have gone so long without your support. You kept propping me up each time life knocked me down.*

*Whenever I had a problem, no matter whether it was regarding my health or my personal life, you could usually come up with a solution. You were the only friend that, if Al and I were having trouble, you could see reason on both sides. Not judging either one hastily. I did realise quite soon, that if problems can be solved however difficult, you taught us to sit and work them through. Sadly, this only worked until there was so little left that it really was unrepairable. Your efforts even then were very commendable*

*I ask one last favour from you Clare. I have left instructions for a collection to be held in lieu of flowers at the end of the service. If you will do the honours of sharing it between Macmillan and Hospice, that will be great.*

*Thanks for everything. Take good care of yourself. I loved you lots my special friend.*

*Bye. Kath.*

While writing this, I have come to the conclusion that all women are, or can be, women of substance. For some this may only become transparent when faced with trauma, such as a diagnosis of cancer.

I cannot close this chapter without a mention of Susan whose breast cancer was diagnosed in very unusual circumstances, when she was half way through her second pregnancy. It was during the late 1980's and recommended management included a termination of her pregnancy, or treatment which would have put the life of her unborn child at great risk. Susan showed outstanding courage in opting for a mastectomy and later gave birth to a lusty baby daughter, now a young woman.

Annie also comes to mind, a single woman in her early forties. She was working as a nursing aid when she was diagnosed with a very aggressive form of cancer. She lived with her elderly father and selflessly approached every decision about her treatment with him in mind. As Macmillan Nurse, part of my role was to ensure she fully understood the potential benefits of treatment and possible side effects. That part was far more straightforward than determining that she did not compromise her own care and chances of recovery in her concern for her father. So much of that is about really listening to what is most important to the patient, and respecting their wishes. Annie, I believe, had been a woman of substance all her life, long before she had cancer.

Yet another woman of substance was Mary, who refused any form of treatment for her advanced cancer, because of her religious beliefs that nature should be allowed to take its course. As a health professional, I found her stand quite shocking and unacceptable. After talking with her about the benefits of treatment, then listening to her as a fellow human being, I came to respect her and admire her spirit in choosing to adhere to her firmly held beliefs.

Each of these women and the scores I have not named,

have all shaped my life in some way and in part made me the person I strive to be today. In their encounter with cancer they found ways of shedding sunshine into the shadows of their illness, so that their spirits live on in those they loved and those who were privileged to know them.

Recounting such stories reminds me that it was the spirit of such patients which again urged me on to take up the cause for the survival of our Macmillan Service.

# *Chapter Seven*

## Help at Last : 1989

*If the sky falls we shall collect larks.*
*15th Century Proverb*

I wrote to Macmillan, not aggressively calling them to task, for I knew better, but expressing disappointment and concern and asking for a meeting.

I vowed to talk with those professionals who were using or not using the service, with the best interests of their patients at heart.

I asked for an early meeting with our Trust's Chief Nursing Officer and it was this that proved to be the most useful, while also being the most difficult. I had enormous respect for the person in post at the time and felt she of all senior staff, wanted the best possible care for patients above anything she ever wanted for herself.

"Your first year's report is excellent," she told me, waving an open copy at me.

"But not good enough to show the need for another Macmillan Nurse," I protested.

"Nor will it be," she raised one forefinger cautioning, "until you record what you have *not* been able to do."

"But the hours I've worked," I tried to reason.

"Uh-huh," she acknowledged, "but we'll let you struggle on until you show us a real need. That means showing us what is *not* being done."

"You mean…."

"I mean you've got to start saying 'No'." She leaned back in her chair, folded her arms and looked directly at me over the top of her spectacles.

I felt myself crumple under her gaze at the thought of what she was suggesting. To say, "No," to a request for help could mean leaving someone in distress. I didn't know if I could do that. At the same time, there was an enormous sense of relief that she understood.

After what seemed a very lengthy silence she broke it by asking "Do you still enjoy this work?"

"Very much," I answered, without hesitation or reservation.

"Then if you want to go on enjoying it, you'd better heed me." She shifted her gaze from me and shuffled some papers on her desk. "Or you'll end up with nothing left of yourself." She had touched a very raw nerve and knew it. As if wanting to save me any embarrassment, she stood up "Come and see me a week today, same time."

Maybe we should abandon the law of philosophy, if a law it is that 'The wise man is he who realises his limitations'. I believe I am wise and do know my limitations, but far too often attempt to go beyond them!

★ ★ ★

A tough decision was taken to close my caseload for a period of two months. Advice on any matters could be sought, but I agreed not to take on new patient contacts, unless in exceptional circumstances.

All departments across the whole District were formally notified. Concern was expressed along with some quite surprising gestures of support and recognition.

The small office out of which I worked was tucked away along a corridor in the Nurses' Home so drop-in callers were rare. Imagine my surprise then when the Chief Executive of our NHS Trust dropped in to greet me one morning, unannounced. While this may be commonplace in some Trusts it was unheard of in ours. With his visit, I began to believe that the Macmillan Service had finally become visible and was here to stay. I did not, however, allow my hopes for an early appointment of a second nurse to rise too high.

The exhaustion did not noticeably ease, but at least it got no worse. I felt better because I was able to make long-overdue bereavement visits. There were on-going discussions around that time as to whether Macmillan Nurses had a role or responsibility in bereavement. For my part I believed that where there had been close involvement with a patient or family, it was essential that there was at least one follow-up contact after a death. There is a mutual need of this and sometimes, there are unanswered questions that, until then, have not been asked.

Such contact also provides an opportunity to offer the bereaved advice on further after care available locally, should they ever need it. I was always saddened to hear from a bereaved carer, accustomed to frequent visits from doctors and nurses during the deceased's illness, expressing deep hurt that no-one had looked in since the death.

I was sustained during my second year alone by several sources, besides my family. One was from members of a Staff Support Group I had started during my first year in post. Any staff involved with care of the dying or with cancer patients, could come along to a monthly forum and share experiences, both good and not so good. As well as providing an opportunity for learning and for sharing best practice, it served to break down barriers by bringing together those working in the hospitals and in the community, in a way that had previously not existed.

I also experienced a sense of valuing from individual staff around the District from several disciplines which I found amazingly empowering. Though I worked with many different teams in any one day, I didn't *belong* to any. As professional friendships were founded, this became less important.

By far and away, the colleague who sustained me most was Hazel. She and her colleague had an office along the same corridor as mine. She was around my age, a registered nurse and health visitor in the post of Liaison Officer, with an extensive remit of arranging all home care for discharged patients from all six hospitals in the district. I had barely known her when I was appointed but soon came to know her as a woman of great integrity, trustworthy and compassionate with a readiness to listen and a refreshing sense of humour. She of all my colleagues grasped so swiftly and readily what my role was about. It was some time before the source of this very special awareness was revealed to me.

Macmillan Cancer Support also contributed to sustaining me. I was invited to attend an annual seminar in Abingdon, for newly appointed Macmillan Nurses, commencing on a Friday teatime and closing with Sunday lunch. I remember comfort, fine food and good presenters providing us with reams of new research and up-dated information. I also remember meeting new people and grasping at snatched moments of shared frustrations about our work situations. One thing I came away with was the realisation that I was not alone in trying to balance all the different elements of my role. What I needed was time to explore this in a constructive way with others who are or have been, in a similar position.

As if heaven-sent, I was then invited to a three-day, midweek workshop for hospital-based Macmillan Nurses. It was to be facilitated by Anne Brown, one of the very earliest Macmillan Nurses to be appointed. She and her friend Val Hunkin started a Service in Cornwall in May 1979 following, I am told, numerous meetings in supportive GPs homes over nuts and sherry! It was the days before syringe drivers when giving four hourly injections was the only way to keep people free from pain. Thank God and medicine for progress.

My kindly Nurse Manager put up no resistance to my request for study leave as I believe she was seriously concerned for my welfare around that time and would have agreed to almost anything she thought might sustain me.

The venue for the workshop was comfortless and stark. It reminded me of my old convent school, hardly surprising for that is exactly what it had once been. Now it was just a convent offering accommodation, albeit we discovered, to those only aspiring to something simple. It was winter and the stone floors of the uncarpeted, wide passage ways and bare bedrooms were draughty, as was the block of half doored, communal showers and toilets. The loo paper was of the non-absorbent kind. The food, taken at a long refectory table in a large dining area, was simple but warming and nutritious. The uniformed nuns about the place, were kindly looking and smiled at us benignly. I found myself half expecting a bell to ring to summon us back to class. It didn't but we did take turns to serve the food and to stack and clear the dishes, just as we had at school. The format and the content of the workshop were like manna, food in my wilderness. Previous interaction with the facilitator, Anne, had revealed to me her unique, enabling skills and this experience only served to further confirm this. I didn't know then but she was to become my role model in my future work.

We were eight participants so far as I remember. There was no set programme, no didactic presentations, instead time was spent skilfully exploring our individual issues, before agreeing a specific agenda. By working experientially, using group discussions, situation analysis, role-play and problem solving, we covered ground vital to each of us in our places of work, in ways that up until then, had never been possible. By the second evening we were opening up to each other, admittedly tired, yet stimulated, re-energised, strengthened and more focused on a way forward. We also felt valued, for we had been listened to, accepted and encouraged, by someone who had been where we were, someone who could truly understand. We had been challenged certainly, by Anne and by each other, for that was healthy, but never intimidated, or confronted.

The final day was spent agreeing strategies for our return. For some that was about meeting with their managers, for others pursuing further education needs or implementing standards and audit. For me, it was about looking more carefully at new referrals, deciding objectively if I was the person best placed to assist, strengthening my speciality, not compromising my role. It was also about caring for me better so that I could continue working in this field; no longer trying to be all things to all people.

Around this time, I read Sheila Cassidy's book, 'Sharing the Darkness'. I was convinced that it had been written specially for me. It challenged and inspired me then and continues to do so to this day. Sheila Cassidy hit the headlines in 1975 when she was arrested and tortured in Chile for treating a wounded revolutionary. When she wrote 'Sharing the Darkness', she was working in Palliative Care and tells of her struggles with the tensions of gift of self in the front line of caring and the problems of overwork. In the following passage, she discusses the needs of carers to accept our limitations:

> 'Is it really the will of God that we should deny our humanity and work ourselves into the ground? I suspect not. I am not talking about times of disaster or emergency – then surely we are all called to push ourselves to the limits of endurance. No – I am talking of routine day to day care of the sick, the handicapped or the otherwise disadvantaged. If we are to be engaged in this work for a substantial number of years then we must take time out, each

day, each week and each year. We must take days off and holidays, like the rest of men and women because, however dedicated, we remain just that: ordinary men and women.

Knowing one's needs is integral to the humility of the carer.'

★   ★   ★

In mid 1989, when Nurse Management requested a six month update on the last Annual Report, this again highlighted the enormous stress the service was under with only one nurse in post. For two months out of the six, the caseload had been closed; credibility was lost during periods of study or annual leave when total shutdown occurred.

In further attempts to highlight the acceptance of the service and need for its expansion, a Questionnaire in October 1989 was issued to GPs and District Nurses, Hospital Doctors and Nurses, and Family Carers the findings of which confirmed overwhelmingly, recognition of the service and the need for a second Macmillan Nurse.

*A Colleague at Last: 1990*

While the above findings were being scrutinised, District Nurse establishment was increased, opening the way for the District Management Team to approve the appointment of a second Macmillan Nurse.

Sister Hazel Tandy was appointed on Feb 1st 1990 and took up post in the April. The aim of the Service was amended to include 'to improve care of the patient with cancer at any stage of their illness.'

Now we were two and our Macmillan role was evolving from a focus on those with advanced disease to one where we could be called upon at time of a diagnosis of cancer.

I remember well the enormous relief I felt around that time; a feeling I can only equate to one that a drowning person must feel when thrown a lifeline. I am not a strong swimmer and am prone to panic when out of my depth. So many times over the past two and a half years while working alone, I knew I had come very close to drowning.

# Chapter Eight

## Are Men Different?

*Strength does not come from physical capacity. It comes from an indomitable will.*

Mahatma Gandhi. *1869-1948*

I have often heard it said that men make terrible patients but I really cannot agree with such a generalisation. That there is a difference between men and women is hardly debatable, from a cellular to societal level. Historically, men have gone to war, women have stayed at home. Women have borne children, men have been the bread-winners. Some of this has changed with the liberalisation of women, role reversal and ever increasing acceptability of house-husbands. One of the differences, childbearing, short of some major scientific breakthrough, cannot change. Whoever created man and woman, knew what they were doing! It is my belief that despite such changes as we have seen, we still look to our men to be strong, resilient, fixers of problems, shelters against storms, hunters and warriors.

In the face of sickness I believe this can make them fearful and therefore potentially vulnerable. Faced with a life-threatening illness, in an area out of their control, they rarely know how to behave and can become quite defenceless. Whoever heard of a sick warrior?

Men within their own gender are as individual as women within theirs. The fiercely independent ones outside a close partnership will choose to deal with cancer their way, come what may, with or without the support of extended family or close friends. For those within a relationship, the way they deal with their illness will depend almost entirely on the nature of that relationship. Where there is openness, trust, maturity and respect between two or more persons, it is most likely that the cancer journey will be made together in most senses of the word. For the many who fall outside this state, their cancer journey can be anything from a mystery tour of surprises to a passage through hell. This is where I have seen men at their most vulnerable.

Alf was a small wiry man with a taller, plump wife, a daughter of twenty and a lean, teenage son who bore a strong resemblance to his father. When Alf was diagnosed with advanced lung cancer, he became full of remorse for every cigarette he had ever smoked. He became like a man on death row might, relentlessly repentant, full of self-loathing for the anguish he had brought on his family.

As a Macmillan Nurse, I tried to get Alf to see his life as a set of weighing scales, with all his good deeds heaped on one side, far outweighing his smoking habit. I put it to him that he hadn't chosen to smoke so that he would die young, abandoning his family, any more than a mountaineer chooses to climb mountains so that he loses his life prematurely, down some deep and dangerous crevice in a far-off land. But all my efforts were to no avail and even after agreeing to see a psychologist, Alf remained to the time of his death a sorrowful figure, the epitome of forlorn grief.

It is one thing to discourage people from smoking and quite another to tell a person dying from lung cancer, that if they'd given it up they wouldn't be where they are now. That is what had been said to Alf by his daughter who loved him, yet distraught with grief at the time of diagnosis.

Words that were likely true, yet words that had wounded Alf more than the sharpest of swords could ever have done. Words that once uttered, could not be undone despite all the love his family showered upon him. I remember the childhood song that used to haunt me long before I fully understood its meaning. 'Sticks and stones will break my bones, but names will never hurt me, yet when I'm dead and buried you'll wish you'd never called me.'

It is not only about thinking before speaking, but rather about a life's training to keep such thoughts to one-self. I have made such blunders myself in the past and fear I still do on occasion, but if we desire to be truly open-hearted and non-judgemental, we must ever stay awake to such pitfalls.

I remember my last visit to Alf, in the hospital side-room he had requested. He was extremely weak by now and though physically at rest, still full of self reproach. Though his family spent much time by his side, he was alone on this occasion. Sitting on the edge of his bed, I put my hand over his. "I'm on my way home," I told him, "so thought I'd just drop by to see how you are."

"Thanks," he managed, looking at me from deeply

sorrowful eyes. There followed a brief pause before he whispered, "I can't think why you bother."

"I come because I care about you." I smiled at him. "And because I like you."

"You like me?" he said, a note of childlike wonder in his voice.

"Yes I do." There followed a time of comfortable silence between us until it felt right for me to leave. I got slowly to my feet.

"Thanks." Alf held briefly onto my hand. "Thanks for liking me."

As I drove home, I thought of all the times in my earlier life when I haven't always spoken the kind thoughts I have had, and felt regret. Yet now a small joy kindled in me in the hope that just maybe, my few words to Alf helped him to feel a little self-worth.

Often, when as a Macmillan nurse I have been asked to visit in particularly harrowing situations, I have questioned what I can possibly have to offer. At such times, I inwardly seek help with the words of a hymn by J Hewer;

> 'Father, I place into your hands the things that I can't do, Father I place into your hands the way that I should go, for I know I always can trust you.'

I know I have the knowledge, experience and skills of my profession and specialist training, to relieve pain and other symptoms, to communicate in difficult situations, yet if I leave my human self behind, or am weak of spirit, I know I am not taking all that I can. I have often called quietly on my God to give me the right words – and He has – even in times when it seemed there were no words left to utter. At other times, I have come to feel comfortable with silence and to know its calming presence, particularly with men.

When all my professional skills are spent, when I have nothing left in my 'bag of tricks' as one man called it, when every pillow has been turned and every crumpled sheet smoothed, I have also come to know the very real value of just 'being', as a human, alongside a fellow human-being in need.

★ ★ ★

Few men, in my experience, will openly express a need or desire for support, whether that is in the work place, in their private lives or in times of sickness. Neither have I found that they are very good at asking for help or assistance, whether it be moving the piano or asking the way to some place. It seems they would rather risk slipping a disc or getting lost! I used to agitate about this male thing; years have taught me that calm acceptance is far less stressful!

In my Macmillan nursing, I have instinctively approached men and women differently. I would rarely speak to a man about 'emotional support' though I may well be providing it. I would never presume they would welcome a hug, but rather begin with a handshake and allow them to set the pace.

Lest anyone should think that my men patients could have their care marginalized by my different approach, which may seem to some like pussyfooting, let me tell you about Alec.

Alec was a forty-four year old policeman with terminal

cancer and a very poor outlook. His GP asked me to see him for he felt he was in denial and that the trip Alec was planning to New Zealand for the following year, to see his son and wife and their newly born baby, would be too late.

"Have you told Alec you are asking me to call?" I asked the GP. "And what did you tell him about my role?"

I knew this GP to be a very caring and conscientious doctor, but one who found speaking with patients honestly when the chips were down, extremely difficult.

"I told him you were a specialist cancer nurse, who may have something to offer we haven't thought of."

"How do you feel about a joint visit?" I proposed.

"I think that would be overwhelming for Alec," he said rather too quickly. "But do come and see me when you've been."

The old traditional nurse in me was flattered that here was a doctor asking me to do something that he felt I could do better than him. The Macmillan nurse in me was regretful that this could be a missed opportunity to pass on something of what I had learned to another health professional.

My first visit with Alec was extremely taxing, yet painfully fruitful. During my introductory phone call, he had invited me to call any morning for that was when he felt at his best. It was also when his wife was at work, which I didn't discover until I arrived, but she knew I was calling and it seemed they were both happy with that. She had left Alec with instructions to make me a cup of tea and a request to visit again when she was home. Many patients complain about the number of times they have to retell their details to different health professionals, often while in hospital within the same day. This can be very tiresome and while being partly due to the bureaucratic system there is, in the case of a Macmillan Nurse, a need to hear at first hand the understanding the patient has of their condition.

Alec told his story of a tumour being found in his bowel which was 'successfully operated' on by a surgeon. He knew they'd found 'something' in his liver and that he'd had chemotherapy for that.

When I asked him about pain, he said that wasn't a problem. When I probed a little more on that, speaking of 'aches or discomfort' right enough, Alec admitted, "That never quite goes away." We talked about what made it worse or what eased it. He then spoke of his inability to return to work or to stand for long periods.

Because we have come to know total pain, that pain is never just physical, but also has psychosocial, spiritual, and sexual aspects to it, we sensitively explore those areas too, asking in such a way that a person can choose what to answer. Our intention is to let them know that should they wish to, they could raise these issues with us.

When I asked Alec if he felt his illness had had any effect on relationships, this fairly placid man raised both arms and bringing them down, banged his clenched fists on the arms of his chair. "I thought no bugger would ever ask me that!" he cried with pent-up passion. "Do you know that I can't make it with my wife any more?" He took in a long gasp of air, then more quietly added, "It makes me feel so much less of a man."

"I'm sorry," I said, then after a moment's silence, "but I'm glad you've told me." The pain of impaired sexuality is something that for too long has been swept under the carpet, and even today it is not always described as part of total pain. It is far more than being about an act of sexual intimacy between two people, but about what a man or a woman feels about him or herself. There have long been supportive networks for women after breast cancer and for those with facial injury, even now for men after prostate cancer, but there is so much that is still waiting to be done in this area.

For Alec, just knowing that his cancer or the chemotherapy could be the cause of his impotence, gave him immediate relief, for he had been seeing himself as a failure. After talking he suggested he could now talk about this with his wife, to break the chilly cloak of silence that was shrouding it.

While it became apparent that Alec had no wish to face his uncertain future head on, once we had prescribed analgesia which controlled his 'aches and discomfort', he accepted that it was a good idea to bring forward their trip to New Zealand while he was as good as he was, for there was no way of knowing how he would be the following year.

\* \* \*

Some situations are more challenging than others and when I think of Ken, that is what comes to mind. I remember him as a man of unbelievable will who loved life and lived it to the full. He was a great stoic with boundless determination as well as a man of humour and consideration, even in the face of his own death.

"I suppose I could die anytime," he told his wife Maggie, "so I think I'd better sleep in the spare room for it wouldn't be very nice for you to wake up with a corpse next to you."

Maggie's response says so much about her. "If that should happen, I will consider I was exactly where I should be."

Though Ken and Maggie lived not far from us, I only met them around the time of his diagnosis of advanced cancer, when he was forty-two years old. Maggie, herself a nurse, wasn't shocked or surprised at the diagnosis for it only confirmed suspicions she had held for some time. It was not until she requested a second opinion that the diagnosis was made. Still now, years after Ken's death, Maggie speaks passionately about professional lack of concern regarding Ken's intractable pain and lack of any urgency in pursuing a diagnosis in spite of his obvious and rapid deterioration.

Once they knew what they were up against, they were both strong for each other. When Maggie gave up work to be with Ken, he was concerned what people would think, but before long, in his own unparalleled way, he decided he would tell the truth.

"I shall tell them I'm dying," he said to Maggie "and that you're helping me."

We never did get on top of Ken's pain though we did reduce it sufficiently for him to spend time with his mates at his local, wearing his syringe driver containing morphine in a holster, much like a gangster carries his gun. He gallantly, some would say foolishly, threw caution to the wind about mixing alcohol with morphine and strangely enough, seemed none the worse for it.

His determination to carry on was a strength which gave

rise to much admiration, but also made life difficult for Maggie at times, and might have been easier she said, if he had given in gracefully to the inevitable. I know when she said this, there would be many instances she was remembering, but above all that last weekend. Ken knew that time was fast running out when he asked me if I thought he would see Christmas, which was only a week away.

"I don't know." I told him, which was as truthful as I could possibly be.

He had got quite angry with me. "I'd better," he'd threatened me. "It means a hell of a lot to me."

If another patient had asked me the same question I would most likely have said something like, 'That's a really difficult question. I will try to answer it, but first can you tell me what makes you ask that just now?'

None of that for Ken, not then. We had been down that road and exhausted it. 'Don't mess me about', he'd have likely replied. 'Just answer the question and be done with it'. And I had, even while knowing what his response was likely to be. A couple of days later, despite his extreme emaciation and weakness, Ken had got out of bed, taken hours to dress himself and gone to the pub. Maggie remembers how he could not drink his beer for his weakened swallowing muscles meant it coming back down his nose. He insisted she take him Christmas shopping which he couldn't do for when he tried to get out of the car, people assumed because of his unsteadiness that he was drunk.

Knowing none of this, as I arrived to visit around teatime, Maggie was just pulling their car into the driveway and I saw the relief on her face as she saw me.

She was exhausted, near to breaking as she got out of the car and said to me tearfully, "He won't give up. He won't let me help him."

Today, more than fifteen years on, Maggie still speaks with pride of Ken's determination to live until he died. She says the experience helped put life in perspective, that Ken helped her see that petty concerns and worries which can assume vast importance in life, really rarely matter.

I still carry that image of Maggie in my mind in her brief moment of transparent distress on that driveway, exposing the very high price this warm, capable woman was paying for letting her man do it his way. My part was tiny, yet I feel privileged to have been there alongside her.

★ ★ ★

I do remember my grandfather dying, then years later my grandmother. Though I felt sad, by then I was nursing and exposed to death in young people, so felt none of the profound grief expressed by some family members. Since 'connecting' or walking alongside the elderly, I now know such profound grief is normal. Grief is loss and is individual. It is unique and should never be compared.

My much-loved father-in-law died in his 98th year. His family and friends, particularly those closest to him, miss him dearly and while mourning his passing, I do not believe any will feel grief at a deeply profound level. Danny had lived a strong faith all his life and was at peace with his God. His wife and one son had gone on ahead and he knew, as we all did that his time had come.

If you are wondering what I mean by elderly, I used to

mean those who are more than the bible's three score
years and ten, but as I get closer to that myself, I think I
mean those over eighty!   Charles was one such man I
shall always remember, who gave me insight into
profound grief in old age. I had come to know him over
a few weeks during his last illness. When I called on him
in a side-room when he was close to death, I found him
quietly weeping.

"What is it?" I asked gently, sitting up close.

"It's the farewells," he managed. "My wife, my daughters,
the grandchildren. They have only one, for me there are
so many." He paused and lifted his anguished face.

"Each one is so painful."

I knew no words of comfort, but instead just stayed
close, my arm around his shoulders, until he became
calm. "Is there anything I can do," I asked.

"Could you pray with me? For God to give me
strength."

For more than a year after his death, Charles's wife
grieved profoundly. While she accepted his death on one
level, on another she felt only the deep, fathomless agony
of his absence. His daughters felt not only their own loss,
but their mother's grief too.

So it is for many in old age. How could I not have
known?

We do not have to experience everything in life to know
or imagine how it may be. I do believe however that if
we can get close to those who are experiencing adversity
or loss, by listening, observing, feeling, smelling and even

tasting their trauma, we can come to understand better and so be there to support and love our fellow man.

In so doing, we learn so much about ourselves and can even come to love ourselves the more. With more of this kind of love in the world, who knows what could be overcome?

I have long been concerned about that part of our culture which expects men who experience loss, to pull themselves together and get on with life and where even small boys are told when Daddy goes away, 'You have to be the man of the house now'.

During my work as a Macmillan Nurse, when men have cried in my presence, I have never tried to stop them. Tears at such times are healing, whether they are expressing grief, love, regret, thanks or any number of other emotions. When adults in a family have said to me, 'I don't want the children to see me upset', I have tried to help them see that, in striving to protect children in this way, we are only compounding the situation for them. I believe this to be particularly so with boys who are encouraged from an early age to be brave at all costs.

Mark's mother died when he was only ten. While it was acceptable behaviour for his sisters to cry openly, feeling he shouldn't, he had stayed in his room nearly filling an exercise book with line after line of 'Someone's crying Lord'. I remember my anguish on finding it under his pillow the day I was changing the bedding. Now, I thank God that he was creative enough to find some release for his feelings in that way.

Men are different from women, but we need only to

reflect on how different each of the men in these stories were, to realise that there is no place for generalisations. Contrary to popular opinion, some men do like to receive flowers, alternatives are Sports Reports, a music CD, old photos of time shared or, best of all, time; simply sitting, perhaps watching TV together or a sunset or listening to the wind or the rain, often 'just being'.

As fellow human beings, when someone close to us is very sick or dying, let us approach with open heart and mind to offer assistance in whatever way that person or their carer most wants by simply asking, "How can I help?"

# Chapter Nine

## Close to Home

*I keep my friends as misers do their treasures, because, of all the things granted us by wisdom, none is greater or better than friendship.*

*Pietro Aretino  1492-1556*

### IAIN

Iain and Julia first came into our lives during the 1970s when we joined a baby-sitting circle, but it was at a social in a village hall when our foursome friendship really took off. I suspect we broke with accepted protocol that evening by our high-spirited  behaviour. They were soon to bring a richness to our life tapestry, in deeply coloured, textured threads of sunshine and laughter, interwoven with profound and meaningful discussions.

Over the years, as our children grew and no longer required baby-sitters, our friendship continued, sustained by evenings in each others homes, where meals were shared and life's journeying exchanged. Though we were two couples in the eyes of the world, we were very much four individuals; each on our own separate journey, yet in each partnership, there was support of a special nature for the other.   Iain had led a very chequered life, peppered with tales of adventures, which we encouraged him to share and which he enjoyed telling. He ran away from school, later exchanged a monastic life for the army before finally swapping all that for civilian life, where he was when we met.

Over time, it became apparent that teaching computer skills at an Army Apprentice College might be financially rewarding but was falling short in personal fulfilment.

For a time, he and I worked as volunteers in an organisation for the desperate in our community. This experience seemed to reawaken in him a calling to a more altruistic way of life. I remember the evening that he and Julia shared their decision with us. Julia was to return to work as Iain had given notice on his job, and was returning to study, to train as a social worker in psychiatry. We were both full of admiration for this courageous step.

What the Army College lost in Iain, the Health Service undoubtedly gained. When we met up we listened to stories of innovation on his part, told in his humorous, self-effacing way, which we recognised was transforming care for patients with dementia. Iain's drive for best care for all, along with an inquiring mind, led him to scrutinise the care of patients with dementia. Put very simply, his findings concluded that many of those affected were made worse by being institutionalised behind locked doors and by treatment prescribed to render them harmless. He was soon writing papers and making presentations on his work and eventually Iain and a fellow professional, with the full courage of their convictions, decided to open their own Care Home, recruit and train their own staff and open the doors to residents. There followed years of hard work, commitment and dedication; all eventually culminating in a huge success story. In business terms, there came the day when Iain and his colleague could take time out in the knowledge that the special care would continue in their absence. That was when Iain began to have life outside work again.

As time passed without us seeing Julia and Iain, we thought nothing of it and busy with our own lives assumed they were having fun, enjoying life. That was until Iain's 'phone call.

"I've been ill," came his voice and instantly I realised there was less of him, causing my heart to lurch. He went on to describe his symptoms, which filled me with further dread.

"So how are you now?" I heard my self ask.

"Waiting. For results." There was a weak, half laugh. "Then probably more tests."

We went over a few days later. Julia came out of the house to meet us as we parked in their drive. Hovering in the doorway was a shadow of the Iain I knew, aged and shrunken far beyond his 57 years, deeply jaundiced and physically very weak.

They shared much that evening of his recurring episodes of illness over the past year; of specialists and investigations, of loss of appetite, weight and strength, until finally, only that week, his diagnosis of terminal cancer. The doctors had spoken of a possible eight months if he wanted to try chemotherapy.

For days afterwards, I felt only shock and numbness. How could this be happening to our indomitable friend?

It was August 1998 and in one month's time we were leaving England for two years as V.S.O.s in Uganda. Gradually my own bleakness shifted to concern for Iain who had so much to live for, and for Julia and their two sons.

We visited again after ten days and I knew from his deterioration that he was unlikely to be with us much longer. I believe he and Julia knew too. Painful though it was to see him like this, I would like to have seen him again and again, shared precious time; yet I knew from the way they spoke that there were others who wanted time with him too, and that I must step back, let go of this dear and trusted friend. I told them I'd come if they needed me. They thanked me and Julia told me to 'phone anytime. Then, because we had always been upfront with each other, I told Iain how much he had enriched our lives and how much we would miss him.

I believe Brian and I drove home in total silence that day. Sometimes, any words seem almost a profanity.

Four days later, Iain was admitted to the local hospice. When I 'phoned on the morning we left for Uganda, Julia told me he was comfortable and at peace. It was October when I received her airmail letter telling me of his death, less than three months from his diagnosis.

In a subsequent letter from Julia, recalling events, it seems from some of her remarks that Iain made a gift of his dying.

*'With the hospice staff relieving me of the nursing and practical care, we were able to just be together. I virtually lived there and I sometimes think we talked more during those weeks than we had done all the rest of our lives*

*together. There was laughter as well as tears and I almost felt that we did our grieving together.*

*Iain himself was so strong and positive, he gave me strength both emotionally and physically to keep going.*

*I have realised in real terms that none of us is immortal, or knows what waits us round the next corner. So I try to follow the policy 'Do it now!' that's why I'm never home! You may remember Iain wrote an article Living for the Moment. I try to!'*

★ ★ ★

## JOHN and BRENDA

John and Brenda also came into our tapestry of friends in the 1970s. I first met Brenda when we were nursing together on night duty on an Intensive/Coronary Care Unit. I took to her immediately for her unique sense of propriety, veiling a strength of character and individualism, with a captivating dry wit.

It wasn't long before she invited Brian and me to her home where she lived with her farmer husband and two children, Wendy and Michael, named she told me, after the children in Peter Pan, that delightful children's fairytale. . That first visit, I remember John being washed and changed and outside with Brenda to meet us. He was a tall man with a big frame, bushy eyebrows, large farmers hands and a wonderful ready laugh. He had been born in this same house where his father had farmed before him, and was truly a man of the land. He was also a cricketer of some prowess and a singer.

We first discovered his singing voice when we called one day unexpectedly. Before going to the house to see if Brenda was home, we skirted the milking shed, from where we could hear singing and assumed it to be a transistor radio. We called 'Hello' but got no reply. Then the singing stopped abruptly and we heard John's voice calling "Maisy! Over here." There followed a slight scuffle of movement and the singing restarted. By now, we had edged our way to where the voice was coming from and there was John, down on his haunches in overalls and Wellington boots, milking one of his cows while singing his heart out.

Our friendship continued over the years, and when the nurse in me first drew his attention to the mole on his face, he made a joke of it. Yorkshire men are not renowned for visiting their doctor; especially farmers who often treat their animals and their ailments themselves. It was sometime later, only when he developed a lump in his neck, which even then was more of a hindrance to his singing than any likely threat to his health, that he finally spoke to his doctor.

Investigations were carried out and the results showed a malignant melanoma. Pioneering and extensive surgery was performed, in the hope of a cure. John's main worry was whether the surgery would affect his voice and prevent him singing. At 62, he felt there was still a lot of singing to do.

And sing again he did and if it were possible with more gusto than ever. Over the next two years, John and Brenda's lives were often awash with sunshine, except perhaps when faced with the major decision of retirement and vacating their much loved farm home. After some searching, they both agreed, not without some anguish, on a bungalow backing onto open fields in a small village, only a few miles from their home.

Everyone who knew John was anxious for him as he faced life after farming, which had been his constant companion 365 days a year for all his 64 years. He had however, made arrangements to continue by assisting the incoming tenants, his daughter and son-in-law, on a regular basis. Sadly, this was never to be. For some weeks leading up to the move he had become unwell and investigations showed secondary disease to the melanoma.

John's final illness was brief and tragic. Brenda nursed him skilfully and lovingly, for the short time up to his death. She was helped by District Nurses, her family and we, her friends.

Without John, the very life seemed to go out of Brenda. However hard she tried, her valley of grief seemed filled with only long, dark shadows. It was poignantly painful.

Just a year after John's death, while we were working in Uganda, Brenda was diagnosed with breast cancer. She admits, somewhat ruefully now that, at the time, she thought of refusing any treatment so that she could die and be with John. However, Brenda did have treatment and so had to make that cancer journey that she had made so recently with John, without him. She says she owes much to her sister and friends and also the breast care nurse and consultant who were so understanding.

When I ask her if there is anything she thinks professionals could or should have done differently, she replies passionately.

"Yes. I told them I wanted to be with John when they gave him the results that first time. Instead they told him bluntly, in the Day Room with other people present, upsetting him and making me very angry."

Here lies a challenge to all health professionals. Breaking of Bad News is an area where there has been some improvement, but where **much more** must be made.

When I then ask Brenda if there is anything she wished she had done differently, she answers without hesitation. "Made John see the doctor sooner."

I accept her statement and after a period of comfortable silence, ask "And during your own experience with cancer?"

She ponders as if choosing how to say what she wants to say. "Perhaps helping my daughter come to terms with everything, although she was having a very bad time herself with life then."

Brenda's very painful experience in this area, is something I have seen often before in families. Because we are each of us unique in our humanity, we respond to every experience, especially when facing adversity, in our own individual way.

Teenagers and young adults are particularly variable and indeed vulnerable in their reaction to loss, and the more so when it is loss of a parent. This is often made worse when the surviving parent, whose affection and attention they crave, is struggling with their own bereavement and unable to be there for them. If further illness then enters this arena, a young person can totally withdraw, with potential for a tragedy of broken relationships.

Professionals, family and friends need to be alert to this possibility and so think widely, regularly checking out how individuals are coping. I remember while working as a Macmillan nurse, more than one young person saying to me. "Everyone who calls asks me how my mother is. No-one ever asks how I am. Don't they know, he wasn't just her husband. He was my father!" Just occasionally, family members may need to be prompted about how they can support one another during this time.

Now, more than eight years on, Brenda is back into life with a swing. John is never far from her thoughts, and it only takes one of their old familiar songs on the radio to fill her eyes with tears and her heart with longing. I am happy to tell you that she is well and never one for self-pity and introspection, spends a great deal of her time helping and supporting those in need, and has recently re-married.

★ ★ ★

## CAROLE

Whenever I think of Carole, I feel an ache, like an old wound. Even now, more than ten years on since her death, a sadness remains. I still miss her. I just so much enjoyed being with her, even in the hard times when life dealt her unkind blows, as it surely did, I treasured my time with her. I believe we knew each other in a way that few friends do. I first met Carole and her husband at a dinner party in the seventies. Very soon after that, I heard her husband had left Carole and their two young sons. She picked up on life by necessity and became a very active member of the cancer education campaign, WNCCC, with which I was involved. After a few years she was courted by a seemingly likeable business man, whom she married. We all wished them every happiness, quietly hoping that early reservations felt by us, her close friends would come to nothing. Sadly, it wasn't long before Carole was in trouble. These were such difficult times for her, yet I never saw a sign of self-pity, rather a quiet dignity, tinged with reproach that somehow, she must  be partly responsible for bringing this situation about. Her sons were adolescent during this period, and there were times when she faced enormous problems in her quest for normality and her tireless efforts to protect them. Finally, she was freed, a divorce was decreed and she began to live again; and to laugh too, which was music to our ears.

I really don't remember how long it was before she told me she had met someone whom she would like us to meet. "I won't marry again," she told me after some time "but we are looking for a house together."

Carole's new partner was very different from her earlier ones, and we soon came to see his devotion towards her. We also saw our dear friend blossom again in the constancy of his love and care. Just as life was beginning to be kind to her, it seemed particularly cruel when out of the blue, she was diagnosed with breast cancer. Our first reaction was, "Why her? Why now?" After all she had done within the campaign against breast and cervical cancer! Other reactions associated with diagnosis of a life-threatening illness are widely acknowledged and include anger, disbelief, denial, fear, guilt and blame. While most of these were being felt amongst her family and friends, Carole, took it in her stride.

"We've been promoting long enough that early detection saves lives." She told me, "so let's believe it. Mine was found before I even knew it was there."

Results following surgery indicated to her surgeon that no further treatment was necessary. Life was for living and she and her partner were planning on doing that, if anything, with a new vigour beginning with getting married.

It was Christmas time when my fears were roused. It was our family custom on Boxing Day to have Open House, with all our friends invited to drop in between noon and four for mulled wine and mince pies. Evening dinner and games followed for our closest friends, which included Carole, this year with her new husband. He rang to confirm they were coming on the day itself adding "Carole's lost her voice, but she says she'd still like to come."

"I am sorry," I sympathised. "Are you sure she's well enough?" I was only too aware that there was a vicious 'flu bug around.

"She's not sick or anything," he assured me. "It's just the voice. Been like this a couple of weeks. She thinks she's strained it teaching."

My heart sank. I'd much rather have heard that she had 'flu. Though she could have strained her voice teaching, I knew too much to be pacified by that explanation.

"Yes," he replied to my questioning, "she's seeing her doctor day after tomorrow."

There was a sweet, sweet poignancy about Carole that evening that pained me as I looked at her as she sat across the table from me at dinner. I was filled with that dread associated with knowing something fearful is about to be disclosed and being impotent in the face of it. More powerful than anything else was my desire to be wrong. The following day was our Silver Wedding Anniversary and though we had planned for my parents to join us, quietly at home, my father was not well enough. We went with our three sons to visit my parents on New Years Day and, a few days into the New Year, our sons left, one to a new job in Wales, the other two back to their universities. To say I have never been good at partings is somewhat of an understatement. My emotions were all over the place; concerns for Carole as the days turned into weeks, never far from the surface.

I was already back to my full time Macmillan nursing after a short Christmas break and my husband back at his teaching. My father was now very ill and each weekend I went up to spend time with him.

The last occasion was a weekday when I travelled up the fifty miles with my brother Frank. I am so glad we went together for I know we each gained strength from the other. I really thank God for being close to us that day. I believe we were also open to His presence, for there seemed to be an invisible spirit orchestrating events. Some may simply put it down to my skills and experience, but health professionals amongst you will know that they usually desert you at times like this with close family.

My father was extremely weak, yet peaceful, and unafraid though aware death was close. My mother was quite unaware and spoke of his recovery. I could see this was causing a rift between them, which if left unchecked could easily become a chasm. Very gently, I told her that my father was dying. She went to his side and my father asked my brother and me to leave them alone for a while and that was just lovely. My last memory is of him sipping milk stout from a feeder, with my mother's assistance. He died early on the morning of January 19th 1992.

I was leaving home to attend his funeral three days later, when the postman handed me our mail. There was a brief, hand-written letter, posted the previous day.

*Dear Clare,*

*It now seems likely that my loss of voice is being caused by pressure on my vocal chords — in other words, secondaries have developed. I'll know for certain after a scan next Monday, but in the meantime, would appreciate a chat with you.*

*Love Carole.*

My tears that day were for so many; my mother of course, who seemed to have shrunk in the few days since my father's death; for my sister Maureen, our parents' main carer who had been so close and so loving; mostly they had been for Carole, for the dashing of hopes, and the fears I knew this news would have evoked. There were tears too for her partner and for her sons. Some tears were for me, for the loss of my father; there were also tears of self-pity, at the thought of losing Carole. I knew that at very best, any treatment could only be about buying time.

The ensuing months were amongst the saddest and most testing in my life. I saw Carole regularly, as a friend, but also in my role as her Macmillan Nurse. She commenced chemotherapy without delay and though immediate side effects were severe after each session, she recovered in between and was well enough to share a meal out on several occasions. They were precious times when much was shared between us.

It was early May when Carole and Paul came to dinner and told us excitedly that the treatment seemed to be shrinking the secondary disease. The vocal chords however were permanently damaged, but she was being offered an operation to implant Teflon chords, which could allow her to return to her teaching job. I remember how we joked about how much more seductive her new Teflon voice might be.

Few of us who work in palliative care are prepared for sudden death. Carole's collapse and death only two weeks later came as a terrible shock to us all, but particularly to Paul who was with her at the time, and to her two sons who lived away.

If only she had had her new voice; and summer. Even while wishing that, I knew what she might have been spared.

I have a card still, which her eldest son sent us a short time afterwards.

> *There are a million ways for me to say how much I miss Mum. I still don't really know that she has gone. Then I have terrible moments of realisation that I will never see her smile again, or hear her laugh, or get annoyed at me being scruffy.*

> *All we really have now is a feeling, of the gifts of love, support and understanding she gave throughout her life.*

★ ★ ★

## DICK

Dick and Brenda were our neighbours during the early years of our marriage when we were living and working in Uganda. I remember Dick for the outrageous telegram he sent on our wedding day; one that certainly would have been confiscated and prevented from being read out, had we seen it. I well recollect praying that my parents would not understand it for anything other than the language of golfing conquests!

I have so many good memories of him: for making the best whisky-soda a man ever made; for his and his wife's years of hospitality, both out in Uganda and back here in England; how he came out with Brian in the middle of the night, to where I was stranded with two small babies in a broken-down car in a game reserve, and how he knew that I would drink the scotch without soda that night!

I remember his unique sense of fun and the way he used to wind folk up, not always appreciated by the more serious minded, but also how gentle he could be with our small children. I think the best memory though, is when his wife became pregnant. I was expecting my third baby in three years of marriage, at the age of thirty; while they, twelve years married and more than ten years my senior, were expecting their first. When my husband was allowed to announce their news at the New Year party, the pride and the joy for Dick and Brenda was palpable in the celebration by the whole community. When the appointed time came and Brenda was safely delivered, seeing Dick as a father was like seeing him as a whole person for the very first time.

Their long-awaited 'child' was twenty-four and a civil engineer when her father was diagnosed with cancer. We only met her as an adult in the saddest of circumstances, when Dick was dying at home, four years later.

Her eyes fill up when she and her mother recall his courage in the way he lived with his cancer, endeavouring to carry on as normal. They share how he was even driving them around close to the end of his life, only finally taking to his bed a few days before he died.

Getting to know his daughter has been a joy. She is an attractive brunette, warm, friendly and enthusiastic about life. Endearingly, she has many of the expressions and characteristics of her father, even benignly winding up her mother! Dick's spirit certainly lives on. Of that there is no doubt.

★  ★  ★

## JOAN

My life and that of our family has been greatly enriched by friendships, but never more brightly than that of a family we came to know initially as near neighbours.

Like us, in 1973 Joan and George were buying their first house, having just returned from working overseas, and it was their three-year-old daughter who brought us together, by proposing to our five year old son that her mother and his mother should have a coffee together!

When I returned to nursing part-time, we began a kind of child-minding, which involved Joan looking after our three small sons two mornings a week while I slept after night duty. In return I had their one daughter once a week. Hardly a fair exchange but, as an experienced teacher, Joan made little of it. Such were the foundations of our friendship more than thirty years ago.

As the years passed they had a second daughter and we both moved house, while remaining in the same town. For us, they were our local extended family and, while never in each other's pockets, little of any significance occurred in either family without it being shared. We share many of the same values; love of family, of a fairer world for all, of the outdoor and camping, of remaining young at heart; seeing other things from quite different perspectives which makes for some lively discussions. Most Christmases in times past have seen our two families coming together in some way or another and our photograph albums tell their own stories. There are those depicting Boxing Day games of Trivial Pursuits, Murder Mystery evenings, gatherings around a table groaning with festive food or simply sofa–posing with our growing and beautiful young offspring. For Christmas 1996 however, there is only one photo of a Dinner at a nearby Country Hotel on the 23rd of December. Everyone is smiling in the photo but if you look more closely the wistfulness behind Joan's smile becomes visible. I had sensed a quietness about her that evening, but at no time had I suspected what was on her mind.

I 'phoned the following day to confirm arrangements for getting together on Boxing Day and was surprised when she said they would just like to stay home that Christmas. She then told me she had been having investigations and had been given the results only a couple of days before. She had bowel cancer. It was Christmas Eve and our house was filled with excitement at having all our three sons home, and a nephew, yet Joan's news struck like a heavy blow, deep into the heart of all our joy. Why Joan? She didn't deserve this. Why now at Christmas? Hadn't enough of my friends had cancer? I hardly remember what I said to her I was so shocked. In the New Year Joan underwent radiotherapy, surgery and chemotherapy, in that order. There is little in my diary during those months, perhaps because it was too painful to write about, perhaps because I was in denial and writing about it would have made it real.

To the world beyond her own front door, Joan remained positively cheerful and regularly entertained us with skilful relating of her treatment ordeals, rarely failing to find something to laugh about. She made it easy for us.

I tried to be a friend rather than a Macmillan Nurse, imparting wisdom from my experiences with others. I did take her to the Regional Cancer Centre when she went for measuring up for radiotherapy and knowing many of the staff who came to greet us certainly made me feel better! It was Joan's first experience of 'The Treatment' and she says to have a knowledgeable, good friend by her side was so reassuring.

Joan has a very sharp eye for detail and characterisation, which illustrate her anecdotes in colourful, humorous and often outrageous ways. When I told her that I was finding the telling of her story, with accuracy, most onerous, her response was typical Joan. 'George says he hasn't sorted out the real Joan in 36 years, so what chance do you have!'

On a more serious note, when she was told she had cancer, she remembers feeling shocked, bewildered, frightened and detached from the real world, and angry with her body for letting her down.

After the initial shock, Joan wanted as much information about her condition as she could get and found Cancerbackup's publications excellent in their clarity and practical help. This national charity, was founded by a young woman doctor, Vicki Clement-Jones diagnosed with cancer, who recognised the need to provide information and support for people affected by the disease. Of the health professionals involved with Joan, she found they kept her informed, treated her as an individual and gave her excellent care throughout. Her family, friends and colleagues, after the initial disbelief, enveloped her in love and she has said since, that she wishes she'd taken out shares in Hallmark cards and Kleenex tissues!

The very worst parts for her, she remembers, were the one month wait for radiotherapy because the equipment was not available, her adverse reaction to the first  dose of chemotherapy, and the horror she felt being measured up for and discussion with a specialist about a possible colostomy.

Today, Joan still thinks, 'Why me?' yet admits to feeling incredibly lucky when she hears of other people's experiences. The experience has made her even more aware of the effect of life style choices on health and her priorities have altered, in that she feels a need to 'do today' rather than leave for tomorrow. Joan also shares that her personal confidence took a dive and never really recovered but as my friend is a great actress no-one would guess that to be true of her, though I long since learnt through my Macmillan nursing that what a person says they feel is what they do feel and so I accept it. I do know that Joan's enforced retirement on health grounds from a full time post which gave her so much satisfaction left her with a sense of un-fulfilment. But glad to be alive.

Joan is well and living life to the full and in our current photograph album she is the attractive blonde in the little black dress, dancing the New Year night away.

## DENISE

I have on my desk a beautiful, glass paperweight. It is dome-shaped and cast within it are four daisy-heads. It was a gift from my friend, Denise.

We met while working together on night duty on an Intensive Care Unit. She was an excellent bedside nurse, who I don't believe ever felt wholly comfortable with the technology of life-support machines and modern monitoring equipment. She would often be the first to notice change in a patient through her own skilful observation, before any early monitoring alarm. She would always be first to offer a patient or relative a cup of tea just at the moment it was most needed.

Then came the night when, just before dawn, as we were working together admitting a new patient, she suffered an attack of vertigo. Later, after very gentle probing, Denise admitted to experiencing other symptoms, including numbness in one leg, over a few months. Up until now, they hadn't affected her on duty so she had dismissed them, putting them down to tiredness or the way she had been sitting or standing. Denise never did return to work on Intensive Care after investigations confirmed a diagnosis of Multiple Sclerosis. I believe her cheerful disposition played a major part in the positive attitude she adopted towards her changed lifestyle though I suspect it was more difficult for her husband and two teenage children.

Whenever we met up, I marvelled at the way she accepted her gradual loss of mobility and other indignities that this disease can inflict. I remember her excitement when she found she qualified for a mobility allowance, enabling her to regain her independence with a little automatic car which made it possible for her to get to and from the youth work she had taken up and to continue her hand-bell ringing at the Parish Church.

I hadn't been in touch for some time; too busy with my Macmillan nursing. I fear I may even have failed to return her call on at least one occasion. She used to 'phone me and while I loved to hear from her, I knew it would be an hour out of my time – scarce, all too precious, family time.

I was at work one day when I had a call from a Macmillan Nurse colleague from the adjoining district. This was not unusual for we often networked to exchange information, or to report on a patient or family who might be moving between districts "I have a patient here who has asked me to call you. Her name is Denise. Apparently you used to work together."

I was immediately curious for though I knew Denise to be living in that area since moving from our town, Macmillan only rarely become involved in people with non-cancer conditions. After establishing that it was the same Denise, I asked. "How come you've met her?"

"Well that's why she's asked me to call you." There followed ever such a brief pause. "She says to tell you she is fine. But she has just been diagnosed with ovarian cancer."

I drove up to visit Denise that evening. As I battled to find a space in the hospital car park, a woman driver sneaked in the one remaining gap even while I was reversing into it. It felt like the final straw and I remember becoming foolishly fraught, to the point where I feared I would cry when I saw Denise, or before I even got to the ward. I had not allowed for the heartlifting, beaming smile Denise gave me as I walked up the ward towards her. She looked amazing, propped up on pillows, cheeks flushed, and wearing a pretty, flowered nightdress.

"Hi!" I bent down and hugged her gently. "I'm sorry about this."

"It's all right." She smiled bravely, adding good-humouredly. "At least now I've got my own Macmillan Nurse."

Denise had an amazing capacity to make light of it all, to look on the sunny side of each day, to remain cheerfully optimistic. Her husband meanwhile recalls the feeling of confusion and devastation at what was happening to his wife of only forty eight.

Whenever Denise and I met or spoke on the 'phone, after the briefest of updates on her condition, she would move on to tell me about her family and what they were doing, and then ask about mine, never dwelling on herself.

Six years on from her death, when I ask her husband if there is anything he wishes he had done differently, he tells me.

"Spent more quality time with her instead of working." The irony is he did give up work to do just that, little realising Denise would die that same year. He wishes there had been more professional love from health professionals, and more clarification on possible outcomes. He then goes on to acclaim the value of the Macmillan Nurse, who 'was very supportive and not at all intrusive'.

When I asked him if he felt the experience of losing Denise changed him as a person, he told me. "Oh yes! I put a greater value on all life experiences, no matter how small."

★ ★ ★

### *Lessons Learned*

'No matter how small.' Reg's words echoed in my head. I find myself even now, questioning how often I take time just to be. This week, I have escaped with Brian to a favourite haunt of ours on the Northumberland coast.

Together in times past we have sauntered along the wide beaches, crouched over rock pools, clambered up cliffs to watch fast-moving clouds sweep across the sky and seen gulls fly into the sunset. With wind and rain lashing our faces, we have laughed and found shelter in the sand-dunes, then hurried to the Copper Kettle Café to indulge in rich chocolate cookies with cappuccino coffees. We have greeted strangers, sent postcards to sick friends and, with hands tingling, taken turns to fill the log basket, enjoyed the smell of wood-smoke and the soft glow of candlelight; yielded to another glass of wine and eaten Christmas pudding out of season. We have held hands, shared dreams and before sleeping, we have gone out to see the stars and then opened our window, the better to hear the roar of the ocean all night long. When morning has come, ignoring the time, we have listened to the cry of the gulls and opted for an extra hour under the duvet.

I needed to recapture some of all that but recalling the lives of too many I have known who are no more, was filling me with sadness. Until that is, I found the white daisies, a small clump in amongst the dunes. There were four of them, their faces open just as they are in my paperweight. I thought of Denise and her spirit and immediately knew that by turning sadness on its head, I could again find joy just as she had done. Joy that I had known these people, that I am still alive and well and able to rejoice at all around me; able to take time to smell a rose, to touch a child's soft skin, to see a rainbow, to taste good wine, to hear the sound of music, and to speak kind words.

# Chapter Ten

## Moving Back from the Front Line

*I said to the man who stood at the gate of the year, "Give me a light that I may tread softly into the unknown".*

M. Louise Haskins 1875-1957

As a Macmillan Nurse, making time for non–patient activity was always difficult when set against waiting new referrals; individuals and their families often in crisis grappling with a new diagnosis of cancer and its treatment, or more critically, a recurrence of the cancer.

Patient needs far outweighed those of some local working party who thought you should be meeting with them, or a publicity officer who wanted you to attend a photo call. I would never dismiss the potential value of either of these activities in shaping cancer care, but merely say it was another battlefield for me. Such situations will be familiar to the many who regularly face similar dilemmas. Good time management is one thing, but in addition, expertise in juggling should be a pre-requisite to any Macmillan Post in which there are double expectations made of you; the NHS Trust which employs you and Macmillan Cancer Support which has made your post possible and provides on-going support.

This is not a grumble, but something I had to learn to grapple with as a fact of life. I would even go so far as to say that some of the activities I was asked to be involved with, though daunting at the time, were actually fun in retrospect. I am thinking of the time when I was asked to speak about the work of a Macmillan Nurse at a Charity Anglo/Israeli Dinner at the Guild Hall in London. I was told there would be several hundred guests including a representative of the royal family, members of parliament and the Minister of Health for Israel.

When the request came through I was on sick leave following back surgery two weeks previously and at the time, I was struggling, both mentally and physically.

It was by then November 1992. In the July I had completed five years as a Macmillan Nurse, but the date passed unnoticed for other things were going on in my life. This was the year we had promised ourselves that on our youngest son's graduation from University, Brian and I would make a return visit to Uganda. Before then we simply hadn't had the finance, nor had returning to our first family home been considered altogether advisable after two civil wars in the years since we had left.

Excitement mounted as leave of one month was granted, air tickets were booked, passports renewed, health screening completed, essential jabs dispensed and anti-malarial treatment commenced.

It was at that point that the backache which had been grumbling, and travelling down my leg, diagnosed as an arthritic hip, for which I had been receiving physio-therapy, floored me completely. I was on a home visit when I felt it go, actually sitting in a bedroom chair in the home of a young wife and mother who had breast cancer and bone secondaries. I only leaned forward, intending to get up in preparation to take my leave and realised I couldn't. Seconds earlier, June had moved her eyes from mine and was now gazing out of her bedroom window across the dale surrounding her home, lost in deep thought. I stifled a wince for I didn't want her to see the trouble I seemed to be in: not now of all times. For the first time since I had come to know her, which was now more than two years, she had been sharing her worst fears. She had been having sleepless nights and when I asked what she thought might be the cause of this, she had told me. It wasn't dying itself that worried her, but leaving her children, not being here for them.

That day she talked for more than an hour. "Do you think they will remember me?" she asked at one point. "Children have such short memories."

We had spoken about ways of ensuring this with a scrapbook of past family holidays, preparing little keepsakes, messages for special life occasions. Most importantly we spoke about the need to be gently open in answering their questions – never falling into the trap of lying for, far from protecting them, this only leads to mistrust.

June had certain wishes about how she hoped her children would be cared for after her death and she said how talking about it with me had helped her feel strong enough to talk with her husband about such matters. Conversations at such profound levels leave one feeling exhausted and I knew June to be so, as well as myself. "I'm going to slip away now," I whispered, hardly daring to move.

"Thanks." She turned and smiled at me. "See you after your holiday." She closed her eyes.

Mustering every ounce of effort, I got up from that chair and in agonising pain, placed one foot in front of the other and made my way tortuously down the open pine staircase and out to my parked car. I do not remember much about that seventeen-mile journey back to the hospital where my office was located. I do however remember having an ambulance driver peel me out of my car and into a wheelchair where I remained until my husband came to collect me.

With strong and regular analgesia, the severity of the acute pain did subside sufficiently for me to complete that week at work and persuade Brian that our holiday must go on. On reflection, I know my decision gave him a great deal more anguish than I would have wished.

It was an immensely memorable trip and though I was never pain free, it was only on a few never-to-be-forgotten occasions that the pain was almost unbearable. Probably the very worst was the struggle to respond to a loo call which involved getting up and out of a two man tent on the top of the Ngorongoro Crater, at 2am in temperatures below freezing!

On return to UK, I went immediately back to work. My colleague Hazel had been alone for a month, the increased workload was telling on her and she was more than ready for a break. The hospital corridors got longer by the day, the days longer by the week. I managed for a month before finally giving into the pain and returning to see my doctor who immediately arranged an urgent appointment for me to see a specialist at our local hospital who prescribed traction.

The following is an extract from my diary.

*Writing from my hospital bed to which I am secured by heavy weights in an effort to stretch my spine so that the slipped disc can reduce and slip back into place. A month away in East Africa enabled me for the first time in five years to step outside my role. The work has changed me, my attitude and philosophy – much as people who have had a personal encounter with cancer have often been changed. In getting alongside other people in trouble, feeling their joy and their pain, you forget yourself.*

*I have seen the sunshine beyond the shadows of their cancer, in their courage, their endurance, their love. In relieving their pain, I have been told that I have given them back life. In caring, in listening and trying to understand how it is for them, I have been enriched and reminded of the preciousness of life that I have. Have I given too much of myself? Can I do it again but at a different pace? There needs to be life outside Macmillan for self and family.*

*Nine weeks of pain has taught me much; four of those weeks I was travelling with severe leg pain, with my husband always at my side. I know that I have grown in spirituality during this time. Like dying, I believe this to be something you have to do yourself, but you don't have to do it alone. You are most likely to do it successfully when you have someone to support you.*

*I believe this could be the time to start writing my book.*

The ensuing weeks were tough and certainly not conducive to writing, except in my diary, which has always served me as a friend with whom I can share my darkest thoughts. It is also a place where I can record my times of great joy and realisation. Anxieties and fears are often halved when I commit them to paper. The milestones for me during those weeks were the failure of the traction to relieve the situation, a CT scan confirming the diagnosis of a completely prolapsed disc, the operation to remove it, the complications arising from surgery and the oh so slow, recovery. Pain remained my constant companion throughout. I never could have imagined it to be so bad. I do now know what severe pain is and I'm not sure I'd want to go on living if it could not be relieved. The specialist had offered me two years' bed rest as an alternative to surgery and there were times in those days after my operation that I wished I had opted for it.

Though Macmillan Nurses have to become expert in the control of pain and its effects on an individual, actually experiencing the invasiveness of severe pain brings it to life in a way nothing else can. I learned that persistent physical pain could take over your every waking thought. It greys your skies and takes the colour from your life. It saps the hope from your dreams, the very oomph from your spirit so that you slip into a dark place beyond reach from those who love you. I had come to dread the prescribed two-hourly turns by nurses, which felt like being rolled over a mound of live molten lava. When relief comes, as it does with effective analgesia, it is almost unbelievable. The comfort is inde-scribable. You can give your mind to other things, you can smile and mean it and perhaps above all, when night falls you can close your eyes and sleep; when you waken you can hear the dawn chorus again. Yet when the pain returns, all of that is snatched away and you find yourself once more on the precipice of your colourless world. Fears come crowding into your mind, not least the one that the operation was a failure. I know from my work that such are the experiences of many who have, or have had cancer. There was a rawness about me at that time that made me seriously question if I could ever become strong enough emotionally, to return to that work.

A journey to London therefore, at that time, at the request of Macmillan Cancer Support seemed to me an unrealistic goal, even though the event was some four weeks away. It would have been easy to decline and with a very credible excuse. It was Brian, my husband who persuaded me to discuss it with my specialist. "I see no reason why not," was his response. "So long as you travel by train and have someone accompany you."

I suspect word was out there that I was in need of some motivation to regain focus and confidence, for no sooner had I agreed to speak at the Guild Hall than the postman delivered a huge batch of applications for me to shortlist for a Macmillan Post coming up in the region. I was one of a few longer-serving Macmillan Nurses who had received training in interview techniques and increasingly was called upon to represent the Charity on interview panels.

Brian was granted time off to accompany me to the Guild Hall and I know that the experience proved to be a turning point in my recovery. As on other such occasions, I spoke of the work of a Macmillan Nurse through stories of patients and that time, finishing by reading Ellie's poem. I know from their generous response, that it touched those present, but it did more than that, it uplifted me and filled me with a renewed passion to continue in this area of work.

Some time later I was again asked to speak at a Charity Dinner, the venue on this occasion being Carrington's in

London. My talk was strategically placed between the main course and dessert, allowing a decent interlude for cheque signing. The after dinner speaker was that amazing comedian, Maureen Lipman and I remember feeling so grateful to the skilful organiser of the event for not arranging things differently. Imagine if I had had to follow her!

I have made reference earlier to the making of a video involving some of the patients and families known to me. This was hugely time-consuming as anyone ever involved with such activity will know, for much more footage has to be filmed and recorded than can ever be used. For a time, through this promotional video, my face and voice became common property as it was used for educational and fund-raising purposes by Macmillan. I did often tussle with my conscience over time spent in this way, even while knowing that without such activity, sufficient funds would not be generated for Macmillan to provide the much-needed services for improved cancer care. Also, all such activity provided an opportunity for raising awareness about the evolving role of the Macmillan Nurse, from one caring for the terminally ill cancer patient to one involved in the care of anyone with cancer, at any stage of the disease. During the early 1990's, a huge appeal was launched nationwide, with His Royal Highness, Prince Charles agreeing to head it as Patron. Much planning got underway for this, with Macmillan's Press and Publicity Officers working tirelessly to achieve the highest profile possible. There cannot have been a Macmillan Service anywhere which escaped involvement in some way or other.

By now Macmillan was becoming something of a household name. It was rapidly growing and like any healthy organisation constantly looking to itself, evaluating its activities, reviewing its place in the wider scheme of things and changing in line with issues of the time and in response to identified need.

As can often happen, there was a sense among the workforce – in this case Macmillan post-holders – that those in the north were disadvantaged because they were furthest from Head Office in London. I came to hear of this first hand from nurses in the Region, who confided their increasing frustrations, perhaps seeing me as some sort of elder spokesperson. I had for some time had the ear of the Chief Executive and the then Service Development Officer and took every opportunity to draw this to their attention. Too many Macmillan Nurses, struggling with the burden of overload in a beaurocratic and ever-changing and demanding Health Service, were at risk of disillusionment with Macmillan, at the lack as they saw it, of professional support from the organisation. Some claimed they had had no contact since their appointment, except from local fund-raisers who wanted them to attend coffee mornings and other events. Echoes of my own start! When invited to a Workshop, with the venue far in the south, such as I had attended and which had served to rescue me in my early days, they had, too often, not felt able to attend. Service Reviews long since promised by Macmillan had not taken place.

It was not difficult to see how this had come about. As Macmillan post-holders had rapidly increased in number across the country, the workload of the three Macmillan Nurse Consultants, who were the lead facilitators of such activities, had increased a hundredfold and of course had become quite unmanageable. Suffice it to say that supply cannot always meet demand, but I have always tried to be constructive rather than destructive at such times and persisted in raising these issues at the highest levels, drafting out what I felt to be required to overcome this hiatus. I cared too passionately about what I knew could be achieved when Macmillan Nurses worked with others in cancer care, to allow such frustrations to damage their reputation as I knew it could.

It transpired that planning for de-centralisation and regionalisation within Macmillan was already underway. This would take the form of Regional Macmillan Teams to mirror the NHS Regions. They would be locally based to enable an intimate knowledge of cancer services and needs, resulting in closer and more effective working relationships, both within the NHS and with Macmillan fundraisers and post-holders throughout the region. Welcome news indeed!

I returned to work in February 1993 after three months' sick leave. An entry in my diary reminds me of my state of mind.

> *In one week I shall be back at work – very mixed emotions but if I am to continue as a Macmillan Nurse for five more years until I am sixty, I have got to change my work ethos or I shall not survive. While out in the Dales with Brian, saw a house for sale and thought how good it could be to take early retirement and run Bed and Breakfast together, using the No Vacancies sign when we wanted time out. Probably exceedingly hard work, but just now something really appealing about it.*

To have made any decision about my future before returning to work would have been against my better judgement. In supporting the bereaved, I always stress the need to give time to pass before making any major decisions. I knew I had to apply this to myself.

The previous year had been a tough one beginning with the death of my father, then my close friend Carole, plus the accumulated losses in five years as a Macmillan Nurse preceding my own health problem. Added to that was the mingled anguish and pride of a mother when her youngest son (even though 22) responds to a call for aid workers in Rwanda, a country torn apart by genocide.

The month following my return to work, my mother died. There seemed little escape from ongoing loss and yet because her passing was peaceful and within only fourteen months of my father, there was a sense of calm closure and thanksgiving that they had both lived into their eighties, which for me superseded the sadness.

News on the Macmillan front was that the much-needed increase in Regional Nurse Consultant Posts was scheduled to take place soon. Totally committed as I was to this development, I still felt some way from taking the quantum leap to decide to make application for such a role. Yet I sensed deep within me an excitement around the opportunity to influence care that such a post offered. Physically, I was feeling pretty good with only occasional reminders of pain and was once again enjoying walking; our Border Collie, Shadow, happy to have me back in action.

The decision whether or not to make an application when these posts were advertised, was taken out of my hands. In the June, I was formally offered the post for the Northern Region. Despite being partly instrumental in the creation and shaping of these extra posts, I felt uncomfortable with the headhunting style, for I knew there to be other Macmillan Nurses who might wish to apply. I took council with my wise colleague, Hazel and sought the opinion of my husband and sons. They all felt that under the circumstances it was perfectly acceptable and proper, though for me the discomfiture remained.

Looking back, I began to see that, in being asked to represent Macmillan on interview panels, co-facilitating workshops, assisting with service reviews and even the public speaking, along with a few others I was being primed for taking on such a post.

My dilemma now was whether or not to accept. Again, I applied to myself the guidance I have often offered others when facing indecision. Listing the advantages and disadvantages of each option, both personally and professionally, highlighted the greatest considerations. To accept would involve the loss of direct patient and family care, as well as time away from home because of the size of the region, which stretched from the Lincolnshire border with Yorkshire in the south, to the border with Scotland in the north and from the east coast to the west! Positive considerations for accepting were primarily that I would be in a position to listen and respond to the needs of Macmillan Nurses in the region. Part of the new role would be to organise and facilitate workshops for new and serving Macmillan nurses which really excited me, for I loved this aspect of empowering through the valuing and encouragement of interactive learning. Undoubtedly, in this new role I would be doing my part in the continuing provision of best care for those with cancer and their families. Through liaising and working closely with Macmillan, the NHS and other providers, I could more broadly influence cancer services in our region.

I would be taking with me everything that I had learned during six years as a coal-face worker with Macmillan where I had gained credibility to take the voice of the person with cancer and those of their loved ones to meetings at the highest level, where as a Macmillan ambassador, I would see to it that they influenced the planning of future services in both Health and Social sectors.

The changed role would also provide a greater opportunity to affirm, by example, the importance of shrewd and imaginative diplomacy, of valuing others, and of dispensing with elitism, so alien to a Macmillan title or to the true spirit of Palliative Care.

Perhaps most important of all, I knew there to be skilled and compassionate nurses in our district, able and eager to take on my role of Macmillan Nurse if I vacated it and it was this above all else that helped me finally decide.

Telling the people I worked with and the patients and families with whom I was involved was very hard. I have never found partings easy and much prefer arrivals, though I know that like sunshine and shadows, we can't have one without the other.

I took up my new post in the November of 1993 and it is with tongue in cheek that I share with you an extract from my diary after only eight months.

> *More than once, I have regretted taking on this new job. The volume of work is enormous – the issues so numerous – the area too extensive – one feels constantly to be struggling to*

*keep one's head above water. By being home-based I feel I never get away from it. Again in my life, I have a sense of drowning, this time in paperwork.*

Anyone feeling impatient with me is forgiven. What had happened to my resolve to temper my work ethos? Must I continue to behave as a workaholic? It really was not how I wanted my life to be. I yearned to get out of the shadows and back into the sunshine. And sunshine there was in the many Macmillan Nurses offering witness to how support from me in a variety of ways, not least in establishing mentorship or supervision, topical and revolutionary at that time, had refuelled and inspired them in their challenging work.

Relief finally came in the shape of two women and one man. One of the women was a most delightful elderly lady who, in memory of a much-loved brother, very generously donated an elegant house in our area to Macmillan, to be used during her lifetime for the benefit of people with cancer. The man was Keith Holmes, Macmillan Regional Director, who invited my suggestions for best use of the house. It was Keith who was successful in persuading both the benefactor and Board members of Macmillan Cancer Support that the house would provide a most pleasing oasis for Macmillan post-holders, where they could attend scheduled Workshops, away from the stresses of their workplace, at a much needed northern venue. It would also be an office base for me, (allowing home to become home again) and, in time, provide room for a new colleague, for it had been shown that the ever-increasing work load in the large region could only be sustained if a further post was created. The other woman was Pat Kaye, a bright, capable, mature and perhaps most importantly, a lively and happy person who was appointed as my PA/secretary. She really was the best thing that could have happened to me at that stage of my life, and probably to Macmillan. She didn't cure my workaholic nature, but she made great inroads into it. She was hugely instrumental in establishing that house as a safe and happy place.

For nearly three years Macmillan Nurses from across the country came there, often weary and worn and left after a two or three day workshop, feeling rested and revived, renewed with enthusiasm and drive once again to take up the challenge and experience the true rewards of Macmillan Nursing. What better way than this, albeit indirectly, to fulfil the benefactor's wish that the house be used for the benefit of people with cancer? What better affirmation that I had made the right decision in moving away from the front line?

# *Chapter Eleven*

## Beyond our Shores

*However much one may know about poverty and oppression at an intellectual level, meeting the poor themselves is something quite other.*

*Sheila Cassidy.*

During our return visit to Uganda in 1992, twenty years since we had left, Brian and I revisited the houses where our children had been born, the schools where he had taught and the hospital where I had worked. We also met with old colleagues who, having survived two civil wars were with pride and determination helping rebuild their precious country. For us it was a time of laying old ghosts to rest, of letting go, saying goodbye to a land and people we had loved and who in turn had loved us. There was still much to do in the country, to get it back to where it had once been and take it into the future, yet we came away with the sense that these resilient people were capable of doing just that. In the posts where we had once been as ex-patriates, there were now very capable and committed Ugandans and we were no longer needed. It was a good feeling.

There is something about Africa that, once you have lived there, can take a hold on you. It is as if seeds have been planted in the garden of your soul, like forget-me-nots, that once in a garden can never be eradicated, even if you try. Just as early spring sunshine stirs those tiny blue flowers to life, so the whispering of a memory or a news headline can stir those seeds lying in your soul and before you know it, you find yourself once more yearning for Africa. So it was for me.

Two years later, as I was turning the pages of a Nursing Journal, an advertisement jumped out at me. **Palliative Care Nurse for Uganda. Required immediately.** The next twenty-four hours were a real turmoil for me, for surely this was a sign. I was struggling with the new post with Macmillan and here was an escape route. I had for a long time felt that we should be sharing more of what we have in our world with the developing world and what better way than this?

I faxed the Irish Agency who had placed the advert for more information. It took days before anything came from them, during which time I gave very serious thought to the consequences of what I was considering. On the personal front, it would mean being apart from Brian for however long the post was required, or for a minimum of two more years when he could possibly retire and join me. On the professional front, I had just established good baseline knowledge of all Macmillan cancer and palliative care services in our region and had begun to build up relationships of trust with numbers of key people. Also, Macmillan had invested in me with extra training in specific areas.

Rationally, I came to the realisation that the timing was

wrong. Reluctantly but resolutely, I began to quell the yearnings and excitement which had threatened to overtake me at the thought of returning to a land we loved, and sharing with Ugandans all that I had learnt through my work with Macmillan. The incident however served other very useful purposes: it further raised my awareness of what was happening in cancer and palliative care beyond our own shores; it prompted Brian and me to focus on our long-talked about plans to retire early and to pursue volunteering with Voluntary Service Overseas (VSO).

My first opportunity to see something of cancer and palliative care outside Britain came in 1995, when I was invited to make up a team of three to travel to Russia to train doctors and nurses working in St Petersburg. I had never been to Eastern Europe and have to admit to a huge sense of apprehension at the prospect, mixed with excitement. I approached Macmillan management with a request for three weeks' leave and was delighted to get their agreement, accepting their decision that they could not assist with financing the trip, for their constitution did not allow this. My companions were two nurse tutors, Richard and Bob, both working in the speciality of palliative care; one in my region whom I had come to know well, a skilled, innovative and compassionate teacher and facilitator whom I had worked alongside, the other his close friend, equally renowned for his inspirational approach to interactive teaching.

I had previously heard from my role model, Anne Brown, of her trip to what was then Leningrad during 1990, when she had spent five weeks there with two other Macmillan Nurse Consultants with the task of setting up a model of good palliative care practice. The man behind the notion of establishing a hospice movement in what was then the Soviet Union was one Victor Zorza, a Russian émigré, who knew that there was no palliative care offered to the people of Russia.

In the United Kingdom, he had experienced at first hand what it meant not to have palliative care and also what it meant to discover it. He and his wife and family understood in the only way that full understanding can be found – through personal experience – that palliative care could provide dignity, peace and freedom from distress at the end of life and, in particular, at the end of a life cut short by the indignities and distress of incurable illness, in his case, that of his beloved daughter, Jane.

Victor Zorza was an extraordinary man who lived an extraordinary life up to his death in 1996 and his legacy can be found in the hospices and numerous home care teams now established from Arkangel to Samara and Perm to Ulyanovsk. His work and the British Russian Hospice Society he founded could so easily have died when he did, except for the outstanding contribution of a hospice nurse teacher, Wendy Jones. It was Wendy who had seen the need for this course that I was to help deliver and who was organising the event. I felt hugely fortunate to have this opportunity to practise what I preached, in the spreading of the gospel of palliation beyond our own shores.

In preparation, apart from pulling together my teaching aids, and checking necessary health documents, I bought a phrase book and after the initial shock of realising that the Russian letters bare little resemblance to our own, I did manage to learn a few words of greeting. Mercifully, we did know that we were to have translators for all our course sessions, both in the classroom situation and clinically.

The first thing I remember was the arrival at the airport where we were met by Wendy and a man with a very warm and openly friendly face, carrying a bunch of flowers which he gave to me, exclaiming 'Dobro Poshalovat – Welcome!' which had the instant effect of making me feel it. I came to know him as Doctor Andrei, a psychotherapist by profession, who had been inundated in his practice by patients whose altered psychological states were often the result of the conspiracy of silence, prevailing at the time, towards patients suffering from advanced life-threatening diseases. Through working with Victor Zorza, he had come to know the aims of palliative care, knew instinctively what it was that patients and their families needed and shared the same persistence as Victor in fighting with the authorities to get it, while owning a depth of human understanding that met people at the point of their deepest distress.

It was late evening on our arrival and I remember all of us being squeezed into an old car and being driven past monotonous grey buildings until suddenly, as if by magic, we were in a different world, one of soft colours, of canals, decorative railings, statues and profoundly impressive, magnificent buildings. After some time, we seemed to have crossed the city and were leaving it behind for an open road and the countryside, of which we could see little, for the only lights were from passing cars.

Our 'home' for the next three weeks was an extensive, three storey, stark grey building, that looked as if it might once have been a prison. The only relief was its surroundings, a forest of tall, swaying silver birch which also housed numbers of other buildings, mostly houses once of some stature, but now fallen into disrepair with missing or boarded windows, or torn, threadbare curtains. Here and there was a shop, serving the local community, with sparsely-filled shelves of goods such as bottled water, oranges, garlic, tomatoes, tinned jam and Vodka, always the Vodka. The three weeks I spent there were some of the most memorable in my life, chiefly I believe because everything I experienced was so different from anything I had known before.

Though our accommodation was basic and comfortless in adjoining cramped, twin-bedded rooms, we did have an en-suite ablutions/toilet space and a sporadic supply of cold water. The paper-thin walls left nothing to the imagination and enabled us to call to each other after lights out, when the unique and sometimes schoolboy humour of my travelling companions, kept my spirits up and I recall frequently falling asleep with tears of laughter running down my face.

Of my time in St Petersburg many vivid memories remain, falling into two starkly contrasting categories; on the one hand great beauty, on the other a terrible beast. The great beauty includes the spectacular architecture of the Hermitage Museum, the Church of the Resurrection, St Isaac's Cathedral with its dome of 100kg of pure gold and Palace Square, where you can buy sweet champagne in paper cups and sit and watch the world go by. The splendid surroundings at the Pushkin metro station put every one of our Underground Stations into eternal shade; then there are palaces too numerous to name.

Further beauty was in the ballet for which Dr Andrei

arranged tickets, insisting it be a part of our visit to his country. We dared not consider what this humble man of small means had paid for such a privilege and we admitted to feeling somewhat awestruck as we entered The Mally Theatre, second only to The Miriinsky (former Kirov). It was here, in spectacular surroundings hosting an exquisite performance, with an audience of extremely well dressed individuals, predominantly nationals, that I began to feel uncomfortable when I considered where I had spent my day. I have never dealt well with extreme injustice and began to feel the urge to make the audience aware of the appalling conditions in their city for people with cancer. At the interval I spilled out my frustration to Bob and Richard, who acknowledged it and between them gradually calmed me, but I still think of my experience in St Petersburg as 'The Beauty and The Beast'.

The 'Beast' for me was nothing to do with our rather grim accommodation or the poor food, nor the uncovered manholes or even child beggars, or the closed, expressionless faces of the ordinary people I sat with when travelling by bus, nor even the cramped housing conditions where it is the norm for several families to share one flat. The 'beast' for me was what I had seen at first hand in one of the state hospitals, out of sight from Nevsky Prospekt or other smart streets where tourists meander, in a building which could have been part of a set for a film of the Crimean war, on a ward where patients beds were so many that they could not be moved, for the tiny space between them did not allow it. What nurses and doctors there were, looked tired and worn and old beyond their years. Some were attending the course we were running and we had each been allotted clinical days where we could work with students by the bedside. I found myself recalling my time in a Ugandan hospital thirty years previously, which had been so much better than this one which was in Europe and only three hours flight from the UK.

It was when I met the patients that I was most challenged. Olga was sixty, paralysed from the waist down as a result of an undiagnosed breast cancer which had spread to the bones in her spine, compressing her spinal chord. Before admission, she had spent ten weeks in a small flat on the thirteenth floor of an apartment block, her only contact an elderly neighbour who had called in on her daily with bread and soup. I shall leave you to imagine how desperate she had become before a Red Cross worker had been notified. Now at least she had some nursing care, a change of bedding when sheets were available and daily dressings. Olga's pain was relieved, but only for periods, for drug supplies were poor and there were not enough to give the required amount regularly. At the time, there was no 'oral morphine' as recommended by the World Health Organisation for the pain of cancer and palliative care.

Olga was representative of many of the patients on that ward whose advanced cancer pain, mostly unrelieved before admission, often had accompanying severe psychological pain due to social and sometimes physical isolation, resulting from the conspiracy of silence surrounding their condition which had permeated their families. One doctor and one nurse on the ward spoke of training that they had received from visiting UK specialists, but felt frustrated when they couldn't put it into practice either because the drugs were not available or the workload was so great that they didn't have the time for meaningful communication. They expressed their desire to work in one of the hospices now established in their country, where they felt they would have the opportunity to put into practice what they had learned.

How well I understood their desire and, while acknowledging their frustrations, tried to offer my own philosophy on this that, by working where they were in mainstream medicine, with the skills they had in relieving cancer pain, they could affect the lives of many more than if they were in a hospice setting. So much of what I was experiencing, in the insufficient funding for health care, the lack of specialist cancer centres, the shortage of district nurses and  the appallingly low salaries for health care workers, I knew to be due to the long years of the old communist system which had been no respecter of human rights. Not for the first time in my life, I felt hugely thankful for our Health Service back home. However, before I left St Petersburg, I did come to recognise more beauty than I had imagined, memories which will stay with me long beyond the beauty of the buildings or the ballet.

During our three week programme we were scheduled to visit two inpatient hospices.

One was Lachta, about thirty minutes' walking distance from our accommodation block. I remember it as a long, single-storey wooden building, extremely modest by comparison with any of our UK hospices. What impacted upon me however was the atmosphere within the walls, a tangible presence of living and professional loving: it was there in the faces of everyone I met; it was audible in the voices of staff and patients alike; it was present in the smell of pine needles and fresh bread over anything physiological or diseased and in the feel of freshly laundered, though shabby bed linen. Resources were extremely poor yet there was a sense of family, of sharing and caring for one another. One young man who had been there for months, paralysed from the waist down by his cancer, smiled radiantly as he told me in good English which he had taught himself by listening to the BBC World Service, "This is the most beautiful place on earth."

★  ★  ★

Two years following that experience in 1997, when I was in my fourth year as a Nurse Consultant with Macmillan and considering early retirement at 60, Brian and I returned once more to East Africa, part holiday in Kenya and part exploratory in Uganda. By this time, we had met people associated with Hospice Africa Uganda, had made contact with Anne Merriman, founder and Medical Director, and had hosted in our home three Ugandan members of hospice team undergoing training in the UK.

We in the western world can be forgiven for thinking that all hospices are in-patient units. This is not so, for though the word hospice in our experience, is generally synonymous with a building, it actually means a philosophy of care and comes from the Latin word, 'hospitium' meaning hospitality. Hospice in Uganda has no beds but cares for people who are terminally ill from cancer or AIDS in their own homes, whether home is a smart, brick-built one in a residential area, a cardboard shelter in a city slum, a rented shared room, or a grass-thatched dwelling in a remote rural setting. Our visit to

Uganda on this occasion was to meet with Dr Anne in the flesh, to spend time experiencing the work of hospice and to explore our usefulness to it as prospective volunteers at some time in the future.

From the moment of our arrival in the capital, Kampala, we were both embraced by the true hospice spirit, beginning with a very warm welcome to Dr Anne's home, where we were to stay. Over the first weekend I went out on home visits with Rachel, a very skilled Ugandan nurse, who was one of those who had stayed with us in England. I should tell you that there are no District Nurses or General Practitioners in Uganda so families are shown how to look after their sick relatives, with Hospice providing medication, meaningful communication and holistic support. A medical student from Europe, spending time at hospice, was accompanying us and as we bumped along in an old Land rover, he would brief me on the patients he knew before we reached them.

"This next one is shocking," he told me, as we approached an area on the edge of the sprawling city where a settlement of concrete dwellings huddled on top of each other down the side of a hill. "Musa is a Somali refugee," he went on "with AIDS and cancer of the jaw. The stench is awful and his wife doesn't care for him." I raised my eyebrows but said nothing.

The stench was awful, yet familiar, before we even entered the building. It took some moments for my eyes to adjust to the dimness after the brightness outside. Then I began to make out a huddled heap on the floor, as the emaciated figure of a man lying in a foetal position on a blanket on the earth floor.

Rachel bent right down to greet Musa and I did the same. It seemed the only common language was Swahili, which he appeared to understand from the flicker of response in his dark eyes. The remainder of his face was covered with a soiled dressing. "It doesn't look like the wife has touched this since we were last here," Rachel whispered to me. Then, while the medical student went in search of Musa's wife and Rachel began the slow, all-engrossing task of removing the dried, foul-smelling dressing, I knelt at the opposite side, trying to hold Musa's gaze while gently stroking his arm, as one might a child. In all my years of cancer nursing, I had never seen tissue destruction of this nature. Where once there had been a mouth and a nose, there was only a gaping cavity.

The medical student had returned with a tall, slender figure who barely whispered a greeting, and then remained in the shadows. "Your wife?" I asked Musa, glad of the smattering of Swahili I had learnt in the past. He moved his head almost imperceptibly, extreme weakness preventing him from anything more. His eyes spoke of deep sorrow, of self-disgust, despair, anger …. and something else that I couldn't quite decipher. Could he be asking something of me? I tried to put myself fleetingly in his place; then in hers and so many emotions washed over me. If this isn't a living hell, I thought, I don't know what is. *Please God I silently implored, show me what I can do.*

Musa was very obviously unwashed. So out of character for an African, for the scarcer the water, the more meticulous I have known them to be. "I want to offer to bathe him." I whispered to Rachel who was putting the last touches to the fresh white dressing. "Have we time?"

Rachel smiled at me, and then asked the wife to bathe him, who immediately became agitated, demonstrating how her husband beat her away whenever she came near. I asked her to fetch water then mimed to Musa by touching his grey hair and mine that I was Mzee (senior) like him, though he was probably years younger. I told him I wanted to take off his long shirt and wash him. After only a moment's hesitation, he allowed me.

After fetching the water, the wife stepped back into the shadows from where I could feel her watching. I had seen the clean shirt she carried over one arm, so as we were completing the wash, I turned and beckoned her and asked Rachel to step away. An age seemed to pass while I waited, supporting Musa with one arm. "Please," I implored, looking from one to the other, aware of tension between them. How could I possibly know what had passed between these two displaced, degraded, desperate human beings? Finally, she came forward and knelt where Rachel had been. Musa put up no sign of resistance as, tenderly, she helped me put on his shirt and position him as comfortably as was possible. Then, as I got slowly to my feet, she remained where she was, close beside her husband.

I felt elated. Rachel asked them if they would like us to pray together before we left and we did so, simply asking God to stay near. Their joined hands and whispered words of thanks to us as we left spoke volumes. Yet all we had done was to treat them as fellow human beings. My journal record of the event reads; *I feel God gave me a great gift today.* Two days later, Hospice received a message that Musa had died peacefully.

★ ★ ★

There were other profound experiences during that visit to Uganda that led us both to a conviction that we could be useful, working alongside this hospice team or some similar project, in a developing country. Dr Anne was of the mind that, between us, we had the skills and experience which could greatly assist in the necessary spread of the specialty of palliative care throughout Uganda, particularly in the face of AIDS and the related rise in cancers. On return to UK that summer, we were both changed in ways that perhaps some of our family and friends found hard to grasp.

Amongst those who did most understand were our three sons, whose own lives were taking off in different directions, both exciting and daunting which included for one, celebrating an engagement and a new job, for another a new job and back surgery! Yet they were always eager to hear our hopes too.

At the end of June the following year, I retired from my role as Macmillan Regional Nurse Consultant. The experience had been a tiring, taxing yet rewarding one, that last sentiment becoming clearer as my departure came closer. I had few regrets and felt anyway that I had done my best. As ever, I remembered best where I had achieved least.

The quite unexpected, prestigious award of the Macmillan Gold Medal was overwhelming and deeply humbling, as I found it hard to imagine I was worthy. It was presented to me in the presence of so many colleagues, but most meaningful to, me, Brian and our eldest son were there too.

When I look now, nine years on, at the photograph of me receiving the medal from HRH The Duchess of

Kent, I recall what she once said of Macmillan Nurses, that they should undertake their role with Love, Skill, Compassion and Wise Council. I hope if she were to know of my work since then, that she would feel that I had taken those very gifts and continued to use them, sharing them with others in a land beyond our shores.

# Chapter Twelve

## The Holistic Approach:
### Orthodox and Complementary Therapies Working Together

> *As long as you derive inner help and comfort from anything, keep it.*
>
> Mahatma Gandhi. *1869-1948*

Over my years as a Macmillan Nurse and many times since, I have been asked about alternative or complementary therapies. An image that always comes to mind is of one desperate woman with advanced disease who took on everything suggested to her, until her every waking moment was taken up with pill-popping, fruit and vegetable juicing and self-administered enemas. Little wonder that her bewildered husband sought help in giving her back some quality of life in her final days.

I, too, felt bewildered recently while researching for this chapter, when I went into a New Age shop to enquire what they had on their shelves for someone with cancer. My initial awe at the selection of books they stocked changed to concern, however, when I saw the titles of two which referred to 'cure for all cancers', claiming on the fly leaf 'Give me three weeks and your oncologist will cancel your surgery'. Others were more credible, being both informative and inspiring. I bought one entitled 'The Holistic Approach to Cancer' and found it to be a much more acceptable piece of work in that it acknowledges that no one can promise a cure. The book goes on to say 'there is a great deal that individuals can do to help themselves', and then suggests a variety of ways. The author responsibly stresses that this approach is not an alternative to orthodox therapy but complementary to it.

For my own part this has always been my approach. When asked about complementary therapies I explore what, if anything, the enquirer has in mind, remaining open to discuss such matters and any experience I have of them. What I feel to be of utmost importance is that people be encouraged to explore and understand complementary therapies for themselves. I avoid use of the word 'alternative' for I believe it implies 'instead of' and consider this potentially harmful. It is the combination of conventional and complementary (or alternative) therapies which results in Holistic Therapy.

The word 'holistic' in this context means affecting the whole person, for it has long been recognised that man is not just a physical being, and that a person with cancer is not just an individual with a diseased body; he or she is a person with a thinking mind and a stirring soul. Pioneers of Hospice and Macmillan have shown us this in so many ways, no more so than in the recognition of Total Pain. This is the acceptance that all aspects of a human being, whether physical, psychological, social, spiritual, sexual or cultural can experience pain which drugs alone will not relieve. Holistic care was never intended to supplant orthodox care, but to be an extension of that care into those areas which are not currently impacted by orthodox therapies. Complementary therapies are commonly seen as treatments not practised or prescribed by 'proper doctors', ranging from established therapies like acupuncture or osteopathy to the less widely understood or accepted therapies of aromatherapy and crystal healing.

It can hardly have escaped anyone's notice that there has been an explosion of complementary therapies of late and a growing acceptance of them alongside, not in place of, conventional medicine. Thankfully, as with orthodox medicine, increased knowledge and understanding has brought about progress and a change of attitude by many. For some time, Macmillan and the Hospice Movement have been at the heart of embracing this acceptance and have extended their services to include such therapies.

There is currently a national debate in progress, with Government examining proposals for full regulation of complementary medicine. Such regulation will reduce the risk of unqualified individuals jumping on the band wagon with a potential for causing harm to anyone taking up their services.

For individuals affected by cancer, wanting to explore

such therapies, I would encourage you to seek out someone who has experience in this field. I am delighted to tell you that in 2002, Macmillan Cancer Relief published a *Directory of Complementary Therapy Services in UK Cancer Care,* which you should be able to access from any Macmillan Service.

In my own home area, there is a Cancer Help Centre offering complementary therapies which was founded during my early years as a Macmillan Nurse some 18 years ago. I felt a visit to this centre was long overdue and recently went along to spend the day there. It is open two Saturdays every month; the venue is in quiet surroundings away from a busy town centre and is accessible, clearly signposted, warm and welcoming. I arrived by arrangement before the scheduled opening hour for clients, to find some six to eight men and women helpers preparing for the day. One manned a reception table, another was preparing an area for artwork, there was one busy in the kitchen annex, two others were quietly talking as they set out books and leaflets and one or two others were busy around the place, setting up chairs and screens.

I was greeted warmly by the co-ordinator who knew of my visit. She invited me to wear a name badge, and then introduced as a 'healer' a cheerful male helper who had approached us. At my prompting they both shared a little about themselves and, in particular, what had brought them to be involved with the Centre. One had had cancer, the other had not, but had been moved to help as a result of life events. They explained that they never knew how many clients would turn up on any day, for no prior appointment was necessary.

In no time at all, I became aware that 'clients' or 'guests' were arriving, so I stepped aside to sit at one of the circular tables, where a helper came over to offer tea or coffee. She told me she came along to help and to offer Indian Head Massage, which I admitted I knew nothing about. A man joined us, introducing himself as another 'healer'. I was curious and, upon questioning, learned that there would be three there that day and that 'No,' they were not all members of a religious group, but had recognised in themselves something that enabled them to be channels for healing. I was touched by the very ordinariness of these men and women and also by their humility.

Shortly, we were all invited to move into an adjoining hall where we sat at one end in a circle of chairs; a quick count came to twenty-seven, including helpers. Since entering the building, I had never felt anything but a sense of ease and comfort, and a natural curiosity about others in the group. Newcomers I thought I recognised by their air of uncertainty, and their glances at others, apprehension etched on their faces. I smiled at anyone whose eyes met mine – willing them reassurance and encouragement or, I hope, for those where neither was necessary, just a smile of friendship in the common cause for which we were there. One of the helpers introduced himself and then led us sensitively through a short relaxation session, after which we were each of us introduced by first name and either as a helper, a regular,

a newcomer, a student counsellor or in my case, an 'ex
Macmillan Nurse who has come along to see how we
are doing'. We were given an outline of the day's
activities with details of therapies available, including
consultations with a counsellor and a nutritionist. A
timetable to accommodate requests was drawn up.

The group counselling session which I joined with new
clients, in a quiet side room, sensitively encouraged
disclosure, the counsellor responding skilfully and
compassionately in such a way that I was able to watch
as anger and anxiety dissipated before my eyes.

A hot lunch of home-cooked and wholesome vegetarian
food brought us all together again, some talking easily,
sharing what they had been doing, others quietly
pensive, the mood of each, respected. I sat next to a
former nursing colleague who had been involved since
the Centre's inception, which was no surprise to me for
she had always been encouraging and valuing, particularly in the difficult days of establishing the Macmillan
Service. Following lunch, individuals drifted to this area
or that, in response to their wishes. A little group of
regulars had dropped in and sat quietly talking with
three medical students who were there as part of their
mandatory curriculum – a welcoming leap forward in
narrowing the gap between conventional and complementary medicine. Soft music played in the background,
broken now and again by quiet laughter or the sound of
crockery from the kitchen. Two clients rested in sun
loungers covered with blankets, both items brought in by
helpers.

I did manage a short consultation with the nutritionist in a gap on the timetable between her clients. I had a request for information on behalf of a friend, about pomegranates which even at the time seemed a bit of a tall order. The nutritionist was charming and helpful with a wealth of knowledge on an almost overwhelming number of natural diet supplements. She made many suggestions which I hoped might be an inducement to my friend to go along and meet her, when more time is available and advice of a personal nature will be more appropriate.

I accepted a thirty minute slot for some Reiki healing from a warm, middle-aged woman who attended with her husband as helpers, for they both wanted to give something back after his experience with cancer some years back. Reiki is a form of touch therapy in which the therapist uses both the laying on of hands and distant healing techniques. It was introduced at the turn of the nineteenth century by a Japanese doctor, who developed his healing system from Buddhist teachings and as a result of travels, research and meditation. I can bear witness to the great calming and relaxing effects of the therapy which remained with me for some time afterwards.

The day closed with everyone lying prone, either on sun loungers or mattresses, again in a circle formation, which in itself felt binding one with another, while a helper led a session in visualisation, with thanks for the gift of self and for the sharing in the coming together. In the ensuing silence, I could just make out a suppressed sob from one corner and from another, deep rhythmic breathing of someone sleeping and felt moved, just being there amongst those seeking help and those willing to give of themselves to help others.

# Postscript : 2007

I have come a long way in my life's journey since taking on the role of Macmillan Nurse twenty years ago. Unequivocally, I can say that being a Macmillan Nurse is the best job I ever had. For all the times when I felt I could barely carry on, there were many, many more when I have thanked God for the privilege. To experience, time and again, the anguish of terminal illness is harrowing in itself. Yet to be there and to witness transformation of that anguish into peaceful resignation or acceptance, is truly something glorious. This happens when individuals are loved and cared for in ways that encourage encounter with their own deepest identity, namely their inner spirit or soul.

At quite a different level, in those with very early or curable cancer, as a Macmillan Nurse, I have experienced a falling apart of their worlds as the impact of the diagnosis overwhelms them. Again I have seen, in so many, the transformation when information and skilled support gives them back control of their lives. My own metamorphosis has come about through close contact with inspirational characters such as those whose stories I have been sharing, and their families; individuals who, through their very buoyancy of spirit, have spilled sunshine onto my somewhat serious disposition. Through them I have learnt so much about the preciousness of life.

My colleagues too have played their part, those within the specialty of cancer and palliative care and those in general medicine or other specialist fields, never overlooking the large part played by Macmillan staff, volunteers and committees the length and breadth of the UK. All of those serve as a lasting inspiration to me.

With such inspiration now deeply rooted within me, I have continued my work after retiring from Macmillan, by working with Hospice Africa in Uganda. From 1998 to 2000, through Voluntary Service Overseas, Brian and I worked alongside a small team of Ugandans delivering palliative care in a Home Care Programme. Since then, we have remained involved and return annually to 'roll up our sleeves' and do what we can to help. We continue to receive inspiration from our sunshine people of Uganda who uplift us in our work, with their amazing ability to sustain cheerful optimism, even in the face of dire poverty and appalling disease.

Over the years, to understand better, patients and myself, I have researched the meaning of spirituality through such inspirational writers as Sheila Cassidy and John O'Donohue.

They and others have stirred in me a greater sense of my own inner spirit and the need to be still and listen to myself, as often as I do to others. From listening to myself, from my family and friends and from all those who allowed me alongside on their cancer journeys, I have come to know the power of the gentle language of truth, the many vagaries of human need and passion; and the oh so fragile vulnerability of love for self and for others.

Above all, I have come to face and accept the certainty of my own death, and more poignantly, that of those I love most dearly. So now I take each day and at some point in it think of it as my last. Strangely enough that doesn't make me sad but makes me smile, for it reminds me that I am still alive and still have unfinished tasks and if I want to get them done, I'd better get down to it. More importantly, I want to make time, not forever 'doing' but just 'being', in the gift I still have of the 'present'.

*'This is what Yahweh asks of you*
*That you act justly, that you love tenderly*
*That you walk humbly, with your God.'*

**Micah 6:8**

# Appendix One

## Lessons Learned

### *Doing what we can*

In my journey through life, I have come to believe that the things which happen to us shape who we become, by the way we are able to deal with them. That ability I believe depends on who we are at the time they happen to us, which in turn depends on our previous experience and how that has shaped us so far. While all of that may seem very obvious, I don't believe we acknowledge it as often as we should. It makes parenting, environment, culture and values, of the very utmost importance.

Roma's death could have become for me a haunting nightmare. Instead it became a beacon of light keeping aflame my passion, to improve care for the dying and those with cancer.

Like the young Douglas Macmillan, there are others who, because of their own personal encounters, have championed causes too numerous to name. I do not believe, however, that one must wait, like a chrysalis, for some adversity to befall us before we take wing to do something we feel moved to do, however small or large that may be.

When individuals are faced with a serious illness like cancer, some describe this as a life-changing experience, which may mean for some that, for the first time in their lives, they begin to make every day count, appreciating every moment, taking from it and giving to it everything they can. Still others break free from whatever they feel has been holding them back from living fully. It is people like these who have inspired me to try to live by a quotation that, for years, I have used in my teaching. 'Whatever you can do – or dream that you can, begin it. Boldness has genius, power and magic in it, begin it now!' Johan Wolfgang Von Goethe 1749-1832.

## *Self-worth*

It was during my Years in the Foothills, when so many people who consider themselves 'insignificant' assisted me on my journey, that I adopted the Chinese Proverb 'Bloom where you are planted'. While working as a health professional to improve care for people with cancer and for the dying, one comes into contact with a whole diversity of people; doctors and nurses, porters, administrators and fundraisers to name only a few. Too often, I have heard 'I'm only an auxiliary' or 'He's just a technician' almost apologetically, or worse, derogatively. They often add 'I couldn't do what you do,' to which I've always replied 'Nor could I do what you do, but that doesn't make your job lesser than mine.'

Though we may feel insignificant in what seems the smallness of our role when compared to others, if we can do what we do with a sense of meaning, then we are 'blooming where we are planted'. Like flowers and plants, humans bloom best in sunshine, the sunshine of encouragement and recognition.

When Peter's mother, Dorothy, lost her mobility and became housebound she told me how useless she felt.

She had once been an active church member and could do none of the things she did before. I knew she had frequent visitors so invited her to tell me about them and without breaking confidences, she shared how some would ask for prayers for this or that. Not only was Dorothy serving her community in a prayerful way, she was providing a quiet place where they could unburden in confidence, a rare commodity in our busy western world. I still remember her modest blush when I suggested this.

If it is some time since you greeted your refuse collectors, visited a sick person, enquired after a pensioner, acknowledged an airport cleaner, encouraged your partner or colleague, or split a prized plant with a grumpy neighbour, try it soon; watch the resulting bloom and notice the joy you experience.

## When a young person is dying

If you are involved in any way with a young person who is facing death, please acknowledge that it is a profoundly sad and difficult time.

You are likely to be seeing or feeling some of the reactions one experiences at such a time: shock, anger, disbelief, denial, fear, or a deep sadness and for some, depression. You could so easily be overwhelmed by it all.

Whatever your place in the scenario, try saying to yourself 'However much I want to, I cannot stop what is happening here', then pause to consider what part you can play to make the best of this situation for others involved. Each one of us has something to offer. If you are in a position to do so, remember to ask family members and close friends how they are. Accept that some will still be hanging on to hopes of a recovery and that, for them, is their coping strategy, even while at a different level they accept the inevitable. Like their loved one facing death, they will welcome any gesture of compassion and care. If for whatever reason you can't be there alongside the anguish, then consider doing something practical to show you care. Offer to collect or take other children to school, prepare a meal or bake a cake, be available to collect shopping or prescriptions, take away clothes for ironing. If you live far away and want to phone but are fearful of intruding, don't do nothing but send flowers or a card, not with Get well Wishes; better a blank card 'Thinking of you at this time.'

If you are a parent, you may be so engulfed in your own grief and pain that you are unaware of how it is for your partner or other children. Even when aware, you may find you just can't be there for them, even to the extent that a distance develops between you at the very time you need each other most. Find a confidant to express these feelings. Try to find a way to talk as a family about how it is for each of you. If this is unimaginable, then seek the assistance of a trusted person so that each member can become a resource rather than a burden. Imagine, if you will, a twelve year old boy sitting keeping watch at his dying sister's bedside. Imagine a father lovingly dressing the disfigured face of his beautiful daughter. I have seen both.

Above all else, whoever you are and however you coped, or are coping now, recognise your own humanity and be gentle with yourself.

## Maintaining Hope

This can feel impossible when the oncologist says, "I've come to the end of what I have to offer," or when a cancer returns or spreads, even before the oncologist's opinion has been sought. This is when it is important to take time in bite-size pieces, for then it becomes manageable. By all means talk about plans for three, six or twelve months' time but, more importantly, talk also about short term hopes too.

For those facing long regimes of treatment, some are helped by words attributed to Mao's Long March 'If you fail, then you try again, and if you fail again, then again you try, and you keep on trying, that is all.' Living with cancer, you have to learn to pick yourself up, dust yourself down and start all over again. For those who are very sick or debilitated this can seem very hard, so here are some ideas which I have seen put to use: bringing forward a long desired visit to some special place; purchasing a new item of clothing; writing a letter to an estranged family member; buying a new rose bush; sorting out the family photos; re-decorating a room; having an aromatherapy treatment; or watching a sunrise with a loved one. When you can think of nothing, then ask the patient "What have you always wanted to do and never got around to that we might do now?" You'll be surprised at some of the answers. 'Keeping pigeons' one man told me and while his wife couldn't embrace that wish, she did arrange for him to spend time with someone in the area who did keep pigeons! One woman with a very conservative husband, had always wanted her nails painting red, and when she had her wish, became quite animated and went on to arrange a coffee morning where she flashed them from her recliner chair at all her friends who came. Another had always wanted to learn to paint and her family arranged for her to have home lessons in-between her chemotherapy sessions. A woman who had hoped to see the sea again, but was unable, was hugely comforted by a video of the sea which someone sent her.

★  ★  ★

## Communication

I cannot nor will not, attempt here to compete with the very excellent publications on communicating with people with cancer, except to provide guidelines in areas which seem to give recurring concern.

If a person speaks to you of dying, don't try to jolly him out of such talk but learn to recognise fears and anxieties and accept them lovingly. The dying often choose unlikely confidants so don't walk away. When you don't know what to say, then say nothing, but stay close, smile, touch or stroke. I have often been asked 'What will dying be like?' I can only tell them what I have seen and what others have told me. Far more important that I explore any fears they may have and give assurance that we will do all we can to relieve any suffering.

When the dying have images, or reach for something unseen, don't argue or challenge, nor is it necessary to claim you can see them too, but rather encourage the person to talk about what they are seeing.

One of my greatest difficulties arises when it is difficult or impossible to understand what a person is saying. I say sorry and keep on trying. Sometimes if pen and paper are provided, or a double sided board of phrases of needs and wants in bold letters, a person can make themselves understood.

Never forget that hearing is thought to be the last sense that we lose, so even when a person appears to have lost consciousness, it is most likely they can still hear. Speak to them calmly and slowly with simple messages that you know will strike a chord and that do not require a response.

**Communicating with Children.** We cannot not communicate with children. This does sound pedantic but was the title of a training day I attended, delivering a strong theme on the importance of communicating with children, especially around matters of sickness in the family or among close friends and particularly when such sickness is life-threatening. We need first to accept that it is never easy, but there are several publications now to guide us in helping children during these times and Cancerbackup is one such supplier.

Research has shown that many adults have faced problems in relationships, through loss of a loved one during their childhood or as a young adult. How much wiser we can all be with the benefit of hindsight and increased knowledge and understanding.

For anyone who may be wishing they had done it better in the past, please don't punish yourself. Whatever you did or did not do, if at the time you did it with the child's best interest at heart, then forgive yourself, for guilt keeps you inside yourself and outside life where you belong.

## Equipment in the Home

There are so many aids now for people who are disabled that can be made available and which can make caring for a person at home, so much more manageable. I do have one plea however, mostly to health professionals when it comes to hospital beds. Too many times, towards the end of a person's life, I have seen these single units installed, with little or no discussion, in the homes of couples who have always shared a double bed. I know only too well how difficult it can be to nurse a bedridden person in a double bed, and the occupational health hazards involved, but I make a plea that every other option is explored with the patient and their loved one, before the single bed is moved in.

On a related matter, when patients with a terminal illness have to be admitted to a hospital, I would like to see it as a matter of course that family members are invited to continue to be involved with the delivery of care. In today's shortage of nurses in UK, I would think this to be at least innovative, while always recognising that main carers may initially welcome some respite while they recharge their batteries .On a similar note, I deplore any hospital ward sister who disallows a teenage son or daughter to sit on the bed of a parent who has just been diagnosed with cancer, as happened to a family I was working with some years back.

## Respecting Needs

It is not unusual for some people when very sick to have streams of visitors. When the person is in hospital or hospice, staff will often advise or limit visiting to ensure the patient gets time for quiet rest; this should always be negotiable with the main carer, and never in tablets of stone. When the person is home, it is less easy to manage. One way is to appoint a close relative or friend to let as many as possible know the best times for such visits or even a time not to visit. That same person could also act as a siphon for the frequent phone calls. Another way to assist or manage callers without shutting them out, is to attach a notice to your door or gate, for example, 'Mary loves to have visitors but has been advised to rest between 2pm & 5pm.' Caring friends will call again.

Carers too need time to rest or take a break in order to keep on caring. Don't be like me and wait until you are almost burnt out to ask for support. We are all of us only human and not one of us able to do everything, all of the time. Take care of yourself and give to yourself. Try to identify where your strength comes from and seek it out. My strength comes from the God within me, reinforced by those closest to me. When we are with someone who is dying all we have is who we are and how we are. Don't hold back, allow yourself to imagine their pain and you will become ever more compassionate. 'Daring to care' will bring you closer to being truly human than anything else I know. Strength will come to you when you most need it, once you can recognise your own powerlessness and vulnerability.

### *Mementoes*

Most of us want to feel that our life has been significant. This is rarely more so than when a young parent is dying and leaving young children. 'Will they remember me?' is something I have often been asked. This is when it can be suggested that they may like to prepare something to leave; a letter to be read when older, a gift for a special occasion, a recorded piece of music, a small photo collection, or like one mother, a single parent, who meticulously recorded, for the chosen guardian, a list of her children's likes and dislikes, their strengths and weaknesses and their favourite treats; because she was 'afraid that it may take some time for them to be themselves and knowing these things would be a help for everyone'.

On a practical note, in the case of a terminally ill husband or wife, or any relationship where there are divided roles, the ill partner can make preparations by explaining the jobs that will need to be done to maintain the home. These may be domestic, such as tips on shopping and menus, practical, like changing a plug or how to turn off the water, or financial, with business matters or details of taxes or insurance premiums. One couple I knew kept a notebook which included names and addresses of people to contact at the time of death; doctor, family, minister, funeral director and friends. It also noted where the Will and other legal documents were kept and other useful details about the running of the house:  something I have thought would be useful for us to do now we are in the autumn of our lives, without waiting for serious illness to come knocking.

## *Funerals*

Few among us will have been spared attending a funeral by the time we enter adulthood. Our memories of such events will vary widely, depending mainly on our rela-tionship with the deceased as well as numerous other factors, such as age, and circumstances surrounding the death. Attendance at funerals has for me, been somewhat of an occupational hazard. I am sad to say that I have been to many where there has been little or no comfort in the ritualistic liturgy of the service or ceremony. This need not be and I am happy to say that with more flexibility in such matters, I have attended joyful and uplifting occasions even in the very saddest of circumstances. My own father's funeral was joyful and uplifting because we were celebrating his life. It was made special in the way that one of my brothers had taken the lead after talking with each one of us, his family, in ensuring that prayers, readings and any hymns were what we or my father wanted. Only in his final year had I made a note in my diary of his favourite hymn. 'My God how great thou art.' I have told mine to Brian, but with his memory (and mine!) I think it may be time to start that notebook and put it in there, so that all my family know it.

In contrast, Ellie's funeral was profoundly sad while at the same time, somehow uplifting and in parts joyful, if only in the knowledge that we were saying goodbye in the way she wished. Not everyone who is terminally ill can do as Ellie had done in talking with the minister, before she died, about the music and readings she wanted at her funeral. Nevertheless, if the opportunity presents itself do seize upon it, instead of falling into the trap, as Ellie's parents might have done, of denying the opportunity to  talk about such things. Whenever possible, every funeral or ceremony should be tailored to the individual wishes of the deceased or bereaved; so much more difficult to achieve with sudden death than after a chronic or terminal illness.

## *Dying*

I long since decided that while I do not welcome the notion of having a terminal illness, I much prefer it to one of being snuffed out like a candle, as in sudden death. I would want to be able to use the time allotted me for the completion of unfinished tasks, for opening my heart for any necessary reconciliations, for getting closer to the God within me and for telling and showing those I love, again and again, that I love them. I hope too that I could give up dusting (my most loathed task) without feeling guilty, listen to music, read again my favourite books, or have them read to me, and maybe best of all, watch a sunset while sipping champagne whenever I was able.

I would hope to be able in some way to prepare my nearest and dearest for the coming and final parting. I hear the smiles of those of you who know how hopeless I am at partings, but can tell you that I would look to Joyce Grenfell's words to help me. *'Weep if you must for parting is hell, but life goes on, so sing as well.'* 1910-1979.

I don't believe I shall be afraid because of all that I have seen, so long as my pain is controlled and as far as it is possible, someone holds me.

> *'For what is it to die but to stand naked in the wind and melt into the sun?*
>
> *And what is it to cease breathing but to free the breath from the restless tides, that it may expand and seek God unencumbered.'*

Kahlil Gibran. 1883-1931

# Appendix Two

## Sources of Help

*The following is a selection of organisations supporting those with cancer, those who are terminally sick, and/or those who are bereaved, their families, friends and professional carers.*

**Breast Cancer Care**

Kiln House, 210 New Kings Road, London SW6 4NZ

*Tel:* **020 7384 2084** *Fax:* **020 7384**

*Email:* info@breastcancercare.org.uk

*Website:* www.breastcancercare.org.uk

*Helpline:* **0808 800 6000** (*textphone* **0808 800 6001**)
Mon-Fri 1000–1700, Sat 1000–1400

**Breast Cancer Care is a leading provider of breast cancer information and support across the UK and committed to providing accessible, high quality services for everyone affected by breast cancer. All our services are free and include a helpline, website, publications and practical and emotional support.**

## Bristol Cancer Help Centre

Grove House, Cornwallis Grove, Clifton, Bristol BS8 4PG

*Tel:* **0117 980 9500** *Fax:* **0117 923 9184**

*Email:* info@bristolcancerhelp.org

*Website:* www.bristolcancerhelp.org

*Helpline:* **0845 123 23 10** Mon-Fri 0900-1700

*Bristol Cancer Help Centre is the leading UK charity specialising in the Bristol Approach to cancer care for people with cancer and their supporters. The approach works hand-in-hand with medical treatment, using complementary therapies and self-help techniques to support people physically, emotionally and spiritually. Courses for healthcare professionals are also available.*

## Cancerbackup

3 Bath Place, Rivington Street, London EC2A 3JR

*Tel:* **+44(0)20 7696 9003** Fax **020 7696 9002**

Email info@cancerbacup.org

*Website:* www.cancerbacup.org.uk

*Helpline:* **0808 800 1234** *freephone*; **020 7739 2280** standard rate. Mon-Fri 9am-8pm.

*Cancerbackup (formerly known as Bacup and CancerBACUP) was founded in 1985 by Vicky Clement-Jones. It is a UK-based charity, whose mission is to give cancer patients and their families the up-to-date information, practical advice and support they need to reduce the fear and uncertainty of cancer.*

## Cancer Black Care

79 Acton Lane, Barnet NW10 8UT

*Tel:* **020 8961 4151** *Fax:* **020 8961 4152**

Email info@cancerblackcare.org

*Website:* www.cancerblackcare.org

*Helpline:* **020 8961 4151** Mon–Fri 0900–1700

*Offers information and advice, and addresses the cultural and emotional needs of black and minority ethnic people affected by cancer, as well as their families and friends. Also offers advocacy, interpretation and a training and cultural awareness programme for health professionals. Befriending scheme visiting patients at home, in hospices and hospitals.*


## Help the Hospices

Hospice House, 34–44 Britannia Street, London WC1X 9JG

*Tel:* **020 7520 8200** *Fax:* **020 7278 1021**

*Email:* info@helpthehospices.org.uk *Website:* www.helpthehospices.org.uk

*This is the national charity for the hospice movement. They support hospices throughout the UK through grant-aid, training, education, information, national fundraising and advice. They are also, through the UK forum for hospice and palliative care worldwide, facilitating the development of a UK network of organisations and individuals supporting services overseas.*

## hospice information

Hospice House, 34-44 Britannia Street, London WC1X 9JG

St Christopher's Hospice, 51-59 Lawrie Park Road, London SE26 6DZ

*Tel:* **0870 903 3 903** (calls charged at national call rates)

*Fax:* **020 7278 1021**

*Email:* info@hospiceinformation.info

*Website:* www.hospiceinformation.info

*hospice information is a joint venture between St Christopher's Hospice and Help the Hospices. It is a worldwide resource for professionals and the public which encourages sharing of information and experience amongst those involved in palliative care. A comprehensive enquiry service is offered with website and statistical information. Publications include UK and International Directories, a range of electronic news bulletins, quarterly magazine, listings of educational and job opportunities, and a range of practical advice and information leaflets and reports.*

## Macmillan Cancer Support

89 Albert Embankment, London SE1 7UQ

*Tel:* **020 7840 7840** *Fax:* **020 7840 7841**

Scotland and N. Ireland Office

1-5 Osbourne Terrace, Edinburgh, EH12 5HG

*Tel:* **0131 346 5346** *Fax:* **0131 346 5347**

*Email:* cancerline@macmillan.org.uk

*Website:* www.macmillan.org.uk

*A national charity (founded as Society for the Prevention and Relief of Cancer in 1911 by Douglas Macmillan) Macmillan Cancer Support works to improve the quality of life for people living with cancer, and their families. It funds Macmillan nurses, doctors and allied professionals who specialise in cancer care; builds cancer care units for inpatient and day care; and gives grants to patients in financial need (enquiries to Patient Grant Department). Macmillan also funds a medical support and education programme to improve doctors' and nurses' skills in cancer care.*

## Macmillan CancerLine

89 Albert Embankment, London, SE1 7UQ

*Email:* cancerline@macmillan.org.uk

*Website:* www.macmillan.org.uk

*Helpline:* Monday–Friday 9am to 10pm

*Freephone* **0808 808 2020.** *Textphone* **0808 808 0121**

Between 12 and 21 years old? Macmillan YouthLine **0808 808 0800**

*A nationally available freephone information and emotional support service for people with cancer, their families, friends and carers. Provides callers with information on Macmillan services and activities, as well as giving details of other available cancer organisations and support agencies, when appropriate. Macmillan leaflets and publications are also available to callers in support of their enquiry.*

## Marie Curie Cancer Care

89 Albert Embankment, London SE1 7TP.

*Tel:* **020 7599 7777** *Fax:* **020 7599 7788**

Scottish Office: 29a Albany Street, Edinburgh EH1 3QN

*Tel:* **0131 456 3700** *Fax:* **0131 456 3701**

*Email:* info@mariecurie.org.uk

*Website:* www.mariecurie.org.

*Provides 10 inpatient Centres in the UK, over 2,800 Marie Curie Nurses to care for people in their own homes, a Research Institute and an Education Service for health professionals involved in cancer and palliative care.*

*Admissions/Referrals via GP, hospital doctor or district nursing service.*


## Sargent Cancer Care for Children

Griffin House, 161 Hammersmith Road, London W6 8SG

*Tel:* **020 8752 2800** *Fax:* **020 8752 2806**

*Email:* care@sargent.org *Website:* www.sargent.org

Free Child Cancer Helpline **0800 197 0068.** 9am – 5pm Monday to Friday.

*Uk–wide social, emotional and practical help for young people under 21yrs of age who suffer from cancer/leukaemia. Sargent Care Professionals are based at major centres throughout the UK and support from the time of diagnosis. Offers limited financial support to families in need.*

## Sue Ryder Care

114-118 Southampton Row, London WC1B 5AA

*Tel:* **020 7400 0440** *Fax:* **020 7400 0441**

*Website:* www.suerydercare.org

*The 18 care centres in Britain care for patient/residents with many different disabilities and diseases. Each care centre specialises to meet the needs of the local community. This includes services for people with cancer and HIV related illnesses, Parkinson's Disease, Motor Neurone Disease, Multiple Schlerosis, Huntington's Disease, people with Acquired Brain Injury and care of the elderly.*

★ ★ ★

FOR BEREAVEMENT

## Cruse Bereavement Care

Cruse House, 126 Sheen Road, Richmond, Surrey TW9 1UR.

*Tel:* **020 8939 9530** *Fax:* **020 8940 7638**

*Email:* info@crusebereavementcare.org.uk

*Website:* www.crusebereavementcare.org.uk

*Helpline:* **0870 167 1677** Mon-Fri **0930–1700**

*Offers free bereavement support, advice and information to anyone bereaved by death. Has an extensive publications list along with useful leaflets, a newsletter and an academic journal. Offers social contact with specialist services to various bereaved groups. For leaflets or publications list, please send stamped, addressed envelope.*

## Compassionate Friends

53 North Street, Bristol BS3 1EN

*Tel:* **0117 966 5202** *Fax:* **0117 914 4368**

*Email:* info@tcf.org.uk   *Website:* www.tcf.org.uk

*Helpline:* **0117 953 9639** 10.00–22.30 every day of the year.

*A nationwide organisation of bereaved parents offering understanding, support and encouragement after the death of a child. Help is offered to any parent whose child has died, at any age and through any cause, and is extended to siblings and grandparents.*


## Winston's Wish

The Clara Burgess Centre, Cheltenham, Gloucestershire GL50 3AW.

*Tel:* **01242 515157** *Fax:* **01242 546187**

*Email:* info@winstonswish.org.uk

*Website:* www.winstonswish.org.uk

*Helpline:* **0845 20 30 40 5** Mon–Fri, 0930–1700

*Winston's Wish supports children and young people following the death of their mum, dad, brother or sister through a range of services: a national telephone helpline offering guidance and information to families of bereaved children; a range of practical resources and publications for bereaved children and young people and the adults working with them; an interactive website for young people; and training and consultancy services for those working with bereaved families and those wishing to set up a grief support service in their own area.*

I wish to acknowledge 'hospice information' for kindly agreeing to the citing of the above information in part two, from their Directory of 2005.

## Rainbows – From hurt, through healing, to hope.

Rainbows Resource Centre, Unit 7, High Town Enterprise Park, York Street, Luton LU2 OHA.

*Tel:* **01582 724106**   *Fax:* **01582 728102**

*Email:* rainbows.dc@virgin.net

*Website* www.rainbowsgb.org

*Rainbows was founded in 1983 in Chicago USA and came to Britain in 1992 where there are now in 2007 over 500 Rainbow sites. It is a registered charity, and an international non-profit making organisation that fosters emotional healing among children, adolescents, and adults who are grieving a loss, through a death, divorce, or any other painful transition in their families.*

## Hospice Africa (UK)

c/o Dr & Mrs D. Phipps, 16 Arden Close, Ainsdale, Southport. PR8 2RR. UK.

*Tel/Fax* **44 1704 573170**

Email hospaf@connectfree.co.uk

*Hospice Africa is a registered charity, founded 1993, committed to providing, or supporting the provision of, palliative care to cancer and HIV/AIDS patients in Sub-Saharan Africa. It is based on Merseyside, but draws its supporters from all over the UK and worldwide. It operates mainly as a fund-raising organisation, but also provides advice and support to its partners in Sub-Saharan Africa. Their principal partner, Hospice Africa Uganda is a model which demonstrates that palliative care is both affordable and appropriate in resource-poor settings in Africa.*

# Acknowledgements

*I am deeply grateful to the many people who have played a part in the creation of this book: to all whose stories are told here, may this book honour them; to their loved ones who generously gave permission; to colleagues I have worked alongside who helped grow me, especially my deceased friend Hazel, and Martha in Uganda.*

*Extra special thanks go to my inimitable friend Joan for her brilliant and discerning editing throughout the writing of this book, and to my brother Frank for believing in it and, in his deeply spiritual wisdom, for ultimately shaping its birthing.*

*Finally, the book would not exist if it were not for Douglas Macmillan, founder of Macmillan Cancer Support and for all those since who have worked tirelessly to take forward this great organisation.*

***Thanks are due to the following for permission to quote material:*** *Sheila Cassidy from* Sharing the Darkness *and* Good Friday People *published by Darton, Longman &Todd; Revd James E Cotter from* Healing More or Less *published by Cairns Publications; Denise Baldwin & Katherine Harding of Lamorbey & Sidcup Local History Society for information on Douglas Macmillan; The Society of Authors, Literary Representatives of the Estate of John Masefield from* An Epilogue *by John Masefield; Little, Brown Book Group from* Long Walk To

Freedom *by Nelson Mandela; Random House Group Ltd from* God Has A Dream *by Desmond Tutu, published by Ryder; Sheil Land Associates Ltd for an extract from* If I Should Go Before The Rest of You, *by Joyce Grenfell © Joyce Grenfell Memorial Trust 1980.*

*Neither author nor publisher assert any claim of copyright for individual quotations, except Ellie's but would be pleased to hear from any copyright holder whom they have been unable to trace, so that they can make acknowledgements in future editions of this book.*

## *Biographical Note – Clare Fitzgibbon*

Clare was born in Framwellgate Moor, Durham 1938, the second of five children.

She trained as a nurse and midwife from 1956 in Darlington, Ilford and Newcastle.

In 1964 she left the UK to work in Uganda, East Africa in an up-country hospital, where she met and married her English born husband and where their three sons were born. Clare returned to the UK in late 1972 after experiencing eighteen months of Idi Amin's reign. She kept a journal from her arrival in Uganda, from which her passion for writing grew.

Clare's time was divided into full time motherhood with part-time nursing and writing. Her first short story was published in 1982. Sixty were published in the UK, some translated and sold in Europe. She was commissioned by DC Thomson and wrote four full length serials, which were also published in volume form by Robert Hale.

Her published work includes features for professional journals and newspapers and a chapter in a textbook. Clare's latest publication is an illustrated children's book 'Stories from the Heart of Africa'.

During her work as a Macmillan Nurse with people with cancer, she was awarded the Macmillan Gold Medal and taught palliative care in Russia.

Since retirement from Macmillan in 1998, she worked for two years as a VSO volunteer, with her husband, in Hospice Home Care in Uganda, where they have continued to visit annually.

# ENCIRCLING PUBLICATIONS

A small family publishing organisation which donates all profits to Hospice Mbarara, Uganda; RAINBOWS and to support projects that nurture human wholeness in schools and the Third World.

The profits from *"Sunshine and Shadows – Reflections of a Macmillan Nurse"* will be divided equally between Macmillan Cancer Support and Hospice Africa.

**Encircling Publications:**
**86 Station Road**
**Hatfield**
**Doncaster DN7 6QL**
**Tel/Fax: 01302 846532**
**Email: encircling@btopenworld.com**
**www.edupub.org**